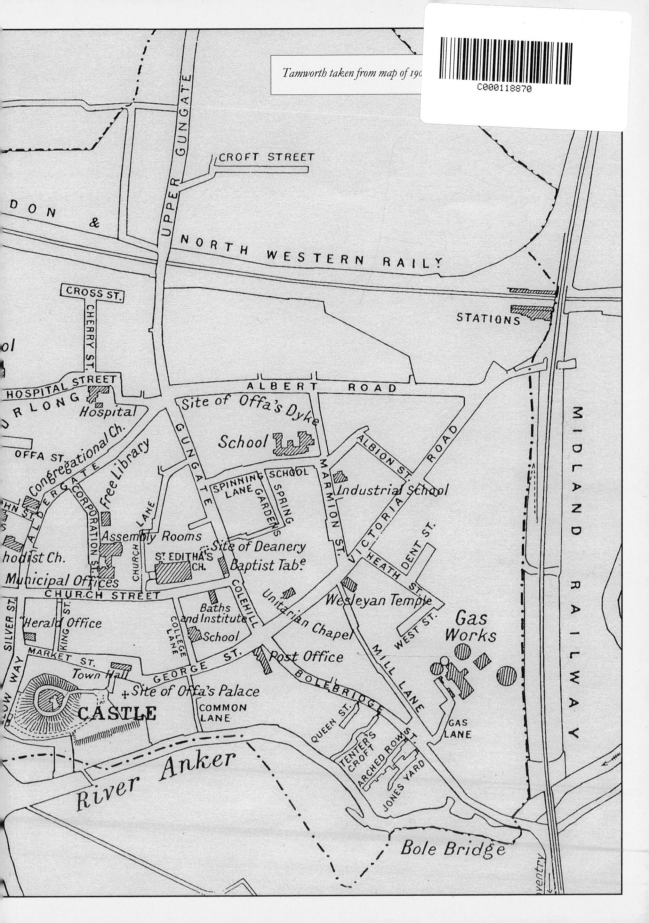

Tamworth taken from map of 190...

TAMWORTH

A HISTORY

Peel statue in front of the old Town Hall by Miss D. Hudson (1961) from the Tamworth Castle Collections.

TAMWORTH

A HISTORY

Richard Stone

Phillimore

2003

Published by
PHILLIMORE & CO. LTD
Shopwyke Manor Barn, Chichester, West Sussex, England

ISBN 1 86077 278 1

Printed and bound in Great Britain by
BUTLER AND TANNER LTD
Frome, Somerset

CONTENTS

For my partner Pam,
with thanks for all the support and encouragement

LIST OF ILLUSTRATIONS

Frontispiece: Peel statue in front of the old Town Hall

ACKNOWLEDGEMENTS

Sincere thanks are due to Frank Caldwell and Sarah Williams of Tamworth Castle Museum; Ian Burley at Tamworth Central Library; Lichfield Record Office; Mr S. Parry, The Reverend Alan Barrett (Vicar and Rural Dean of Tamworth), Mr P. Edden, Pauline Wright, Alec Benwell, the Friends of Tamworth Castle and the many individuals who have been friendly and helpful in the course of my research.

The following photographs and documents from the Tamworth Castle collections are reproduced courtesy of Tamworth Borough Council: frontispiece, 14, 23, 24, 25, 28, 31, 32, 33, 34, 35, 40, 43, 46, 47, 48, 49, 50, 51, 54, 58, 59, 60, 62, 67, 68, 73, 74, 76, 77, 80, 81, 83, 84, 85, 86, 87, 88, 90, 91, 93, 94, 96, 97, 98, 99, 103, 104, 105, 106, 107, 108, 109, 110, 111, 112, 113, 114, 116, 120, 124, 125, 126, 128.

My own photographs for illustrations numbered 5, 18, 22, 56, 61, 63, 100, 129 are also reproduced by permission of Tamworth Borough Council, 22 and 63 with additional permission from the Victoria and Albert Museum.

Thanks also to Helen Stone for line drawings 3, 4, 9, 10, 15, 29; Karen Lanchester for photographs 45, 53, 121, 131, 132; Gary Coates (University of Birmingham Field Archaeology Unit) 1; and Acorn Photography for author photograph.

One

FROM PREHISTORY TO
ROYAL ANGLO-SAXON TOWN

The first humans to walk in the Tame Valley were nomadic hunter-gatherers, small family groups drifting along the margins of the waterways through the wildwood. They shared the land with great beasts. Fossil remains of aurochs, bear, mammoth, woolly rhino and other vanished creatures have been found preserved in the gravel beds deposited over 35,000 years ago when the river flowed deep and wide. Natural resources, clay, coal, sandstone and millstone grit, lay buried in the geological substructure. Stone-Age shelters were most probably temporary huts made of vegetation and animal skins draped over a framework of branches.

In Neolithic times, around 4500 B.C., polished stone axes with fine edges and wooden handles replaced crudely finished, muscle-jarring implements held directly in the palm of the hand. Swathes of natural woodland were felled. Substantial shelters intended as seasonal or semi-permanent homes were built. Farming began but, because it was relatively thinly populated, the land around the Tame and Anker rivers remained well wooded around the clearings.

1 Woolly rhinoceros. The well-preserved remains of a woolly rhino, one of a number of important prehistoric finds made at Whitemoor Haye quarry in the Tame Valley in 2002. This almost complete skeleton is of a beast four metres long that would have weighed around one and a half tonnes when it was alive 35,000 years ago.

Traces of these early inhabitants are rare: occasional sherds of fired clay, a handful of flint chips – the flakes of debris produced in shaping basic stone tools – and a thin scatter of finished articles. The axe was the multi-purpose tool of prehistory. In 1962 a small Bronze-Age axe-hammer was dug up in the front garden of a house in Thackeray Drive. It was made from camptonite, a type of tough igneous rock found in north Warwickshire in the area around Nuneaton. A cast bronze spearhead recovered from the River Anker is recorded in Tamworth Castle Museum's catalogue for 1906. River and water cults flourished in the Bronze Age and this valuable item may have been deliberately deposited as a ritual offering. The people of that time left their mark on the land. Skylined on a ridge overlooking the River Tame at Elford, four miles north of Tamworth, is a round barrow or burial mound. Excavations have revealed a cremation of Bronze-Age date. Barrow sites were selected with care, integrated elements in a sacred landscape. This prominent memorial, perhaps the grave of a chief, may have served both as boundary marker and ceremonial centre. Crop and soil marks visible on aerial photographs show recognisable signs of farming activity taking place two to three thousand years ago in the fertile valley below.

2   *Elford Low. On a prominent ridge overlooking the Tame Valley, this burial mound contained the remains of a Bronze-Age cremation and was probably an ancient boundary marker.*

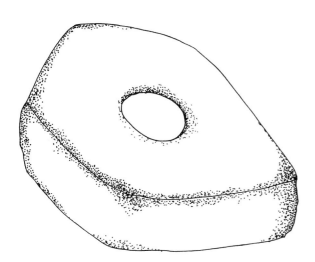

3   *Bronze-Age axe-hammer, the multi-purpose tool of prehistoric times. A rare local find turned up in the front garden of a house in Thackeray Drive in 1962. Measuring approximately 140mm. in length, it is made from camptonite, a tough igneous rock found in north Warwickshire, and is around 3,500 years old.*

4   *Gold-alloy torc. Made between 100 B.C. and A.D. 100 for an important Iron-Age leader, the neck ring was discovered by workmen digging drainage trenches beside the Coventry Canal at Glascote in 1943. Twelve separate wire strands are woven together and secured on segmented loop-shaped terminals.*

A gold-alloy torc or neck ring of the style worn by the most important Celtic tribal leaders in the Iron Age was dug up in a boatyard beside the Coventry Canal north of Glascote during the Second World War. The workmen who made the discovery thought they had unearthed an old coffin handle. It was 1970 before the true value of their find was recognised. Twelve wires, each an amalgam of gold, silver and copper, are twisted in pairs, interwoven and attached to rounded terminals in a horseshoe shape measuring 18cm across. Gold content of the collar is around 135 grams, almost a third of its total weight. The torc was probably made for a local chieftain sometime between 100 B.C. and A.D. 100. An incredibly valuable item in any age, the Glascote find is now on secure display in Birmingham Museum and Art Gallery.

Early Communications

Trading routes for salt, grain and other goods linked the area with the rest of the country and beyond into continental Europe. There were a number of shallow places where the River Tame could be forded, including a strategically important crossing near the confluence with the Anker. An ancient road known as Wendley-way entered the area along the line of Salters Lane, heading for this ford. Holloway, the name of the road leading to this same spot today, is a general term used to describe sunken paths eroded by centuries of use. Other prehistoric trackways probably joined the Wendley-way at Tamworth, one from the south-east via a ford across the Anker along the route of Bolebridge Street, and another to the west where present-day Lichfield Street extends. Watling Street, now the A5, linked Roman London with Wroxeter

5   *Roman pig of lead, one of a pair, 535mm long and weighing 68 kilos, found on Hints Common. The inscription IMP. VESP. VII.T.IMP.V.COS identifies it as dating from A.D. 76, the property of Emperor Vespasian and his eldest son Titus, joint consuls of Rome. Around 24 ladles of molten lead went into a standard pig.*

and was later extended to Chester. This military dual carriageway was a major artery of the empire. A route passing one mile south of Tamworth suggests little here beyond a farmstead or two during the centuries of Roman occupation. Fragments of tile and painted plaster found near Bolebridge Street and a double-ditched enclosure beside Lichfield Road confirm some settlement of the area in Roman times. Between 1792 and 1838, two Roman ingots or 'pigs' of lead from the reign of Vespasian were dug up on Hints Common close to Watling Street. Slaves worked the lead mines of Britain and sweated over smelting hearths. Ingots were transported by cart or packhorse to the nearest port for onward shipment to Rome.

The Anglo-Saxons and the Creation of Mercia

Historians are constantly revising their views of the so-called 'Dark Ages', the period that followed Roman rule. Written records are few. Beyond dispute is that with the influx of Angles, Saxons and Jutes, Anglo-Saxon culture became dominant and sowed the seeds of modern England. The truth is more complex than either the tale of bloody conquest long taught in our schools or mere cultural assimilation. Mercia was the last of the Anglo-Saxon kingdoms to be established, in 585. Under Penda in the seventh century it became the most powerful, controlling an area stretching from the Thames to the Humber and from Wales to East Anglia.

The Mercian rulers inherited a feudal social structure based on territorial units developed from Roman villa estates. A Mercian commissioned survey, the *Tribal Hidage*, which may date from the period immediately after Penda's death in 655, records two distinct folk groups in southern Mercia, the Tomsaetan or 'the people of the Tame' occupying land stretching from what is now north Worcestershire to the River Trent at Breedon on the Hill, and their

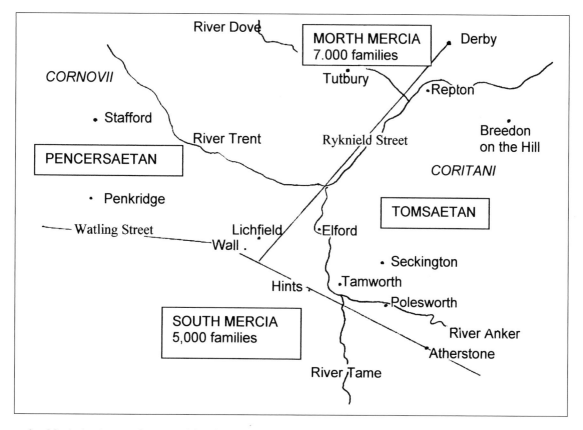

6 *Mercia in the seventh century. Two distinct Anglo-Saxon folk groups dominated south Mercia. The lands of the Tomsaetan or 'People of the Tame' centred on the Tame Valley, an area shared with the Romano-British Coritani.*

neighbours the Pencersaetan, occupying north-west Staffordshire and Shropshire. According to the Anglo-Saxon historian and scholar Bede, writing around 730, the Tomsaetan and Pencersaetan together numbered around five thousand families. This was a time before the country was divided into shires. A 'hide' was an imprecise measurement, based on the amount of land deemed necessary to support a family. One hundred hides made up an administrative unit assessable for tax or tribute. Payment might be in service, goods or hard cash.

Most ordinary people worked the land, part of a feudal pecking order with slaves at one end of the scale, thanes at the other, tenant villeins and landowning freemen in between. Social order was a devolved communal responsibility. The individual freemen of each hundred were required to join a 'tithing', a group of ten men under sworn oath to be collectively answerable for the good conduct of each other.

Early Christian Tamworth and the Royal Palace

Christianity retained little more than a tenuous toehold in immediately post-Roman Mercia. It was re-established after the death of Penda by his sons, Peada and Wulfhere. Diuma, a

7 *Site of St Ruffin's Well, tucked into a corner of the Castle Grounds in the shadow of the Ankerside Shopping Centre. According to legend, Ruffin, son of the Mercian ruler Wulfhere, was baptised after a stag he was hunting led him to the cell of St Chad. Ancient wells often acquired a reputation for healing properties.*

Northumbrian monk, became the first bishop of Mercia. Churches were endowed with land and the details of the transactions noted in a series of charters and memoranda. After the death of Bishop Jaruman, Wulfhere asked the Archbishop of Canterbury to nominate a replacement. In 669 St Chad was appointed. A church at Tamworth is first recorded around this time but an earlier establishment is possible. Chad most probably accompanied his elder brother Cedd on Diuma's mission to the area in 653. The site of an ancient holy well in the south-eastern corner of the Castle Grounds is dedicated to St Ruffin, a reference to one of Wulfhere's sons. Legend tells that

Ruffin was baptised after a stag he was hunting led him to Chad's cell.

Mercian rulers were itinerant. Being visible was an indispensable part of asserting kingly authority. That, coupled with the economic challenge of keeping a large royal household supplied with food, made travelling between a number of residences a necessity. It is possible that Tamworth was a pit stop on the royal circuit before allusions to a royal residence begin to appear in charters. The first recorded mention comes in 781. A grant of land to the monks of Worcester, signed by Offa, King of Mercia, is addressed from his royal palace at 'Tamworthie'.

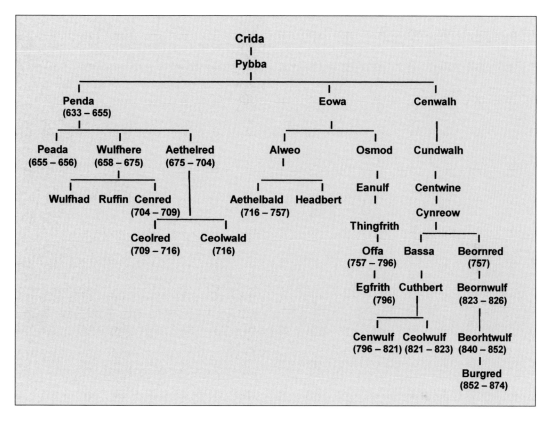

8 *Mercian royal line. Mercia was established in 585. Under Penda it became the most powerful of the Anglo-Saxon kingdoms. Offa claimed the throne after avenging the murder of his cousin Aethelbald and made Tamworth a royal residence. When Burgred fled to Rome in 874, Mercia was divided between Saxon Wessex and the Danish invaders.*

A late seventh-century mention of Tomtun, 'the farmstead by the Tame', in a transaction relating to Peterborough Abbey, may be an earlier reference to Tamworth as a settlement. By 799, there is indisputable charter evidence of the existence of 'the enclosure by the Tame', the first town in Staffordshire since the departure of the legions.

Offa claimed the Mercian throne after avenging the murder of his cousin Aethelbald, killed by a rebellious kinsman, Beornred, in the wake of defeat at the hands of a force of West Saxons in 757. That battle had taken place at Seckington, just four miles

north of Tamworth, and may explain why Offa chose to make his principal residence here. There can be no doubt it was a favourite place. The charter of 781 was signed at Christmas time. Offa was diligent in his religious observance and would not have chosen to spend such an important Christian festival here if there were no church in which to celebrate the occasion. Later kings also issued charters from Tamworth dated at Easter and Christmas. Offa became a dominant force in England, his influence stretching into Europe. Emperor Charlemagne, founder of the Holy Roman Empire, thought it politic to refer to Offa as his

9   *Offa's palace at Tamworth. Wooden buildings leave little trace and the location of Offa's palace remains a mystery. We may imagine a large aisled hall with split log walls, a steeply pitched roof of thatch and, inside, a fire burning in a central hearth.*

10   *Anglo-Saxon watermill. The remains of a ninth-century mill for grinding corn built just outside the borough defences close to the River Anker. Sluices on either side controlled the flow of water, one chute driving a horizontal wheel that turned a millstone on the floor above, the other forming a by-pass channel.*

'dearest brother' and to treat him as an equal. Tamworth's importance as a royal head-quarters reflected Offa's power.

In the eighth century this was a land of wooden buildings. They left little lasting impression on the landscape. Few traces remain. Not even the shadows of post holes have been discovered to pinpoint the location of the royal palace. We must assume a large aisled hall open to the roof beams, split log walls rising vertically from a sill to a steeply pitched, ridged roof. Inside, a log fire burning in a central hearth, smoke curling freely upwards to find its own escape through thick thatch. Excavations north-east of Bolebridge Street in 1968 revealed what appeared to be the outline of a large Saxon building. Other suggested sites include the area of the churchyard north of St Editha's and close to the Market Street entrance into the Castle Grounds.

An enclosure ditch surrounded the royal palace, church and a range of other buildings housing the people and functions necessary to support the king and his retinue. Excavation evidence suggests a modest trench set with sharpened stakes pointing outwards, as much status symbol or animal deterrent as serious military barricade.

Anglo-Saxon Tamworth was largely self-sufficient. A rare find of well-preserved timbers excavated beside the River Anker behind Bolebridge Street just outside the defences turned out to be the remains of two watermills. The first had been built over a specially constructed mill-race that channelled water from the river below a clay dam. A later two-storey replacement on the site had a mill-pond fed from a leat. A horizontal waterwheel in the mill basement turned a drive shaft connected to grind-stones on the ground floor directly above the wheel. Corn was fed between the stones via a hopper. The upper millstone rotated with the action of the wheel and was adjustable, allowing the gap between the stones to be set to produce either fine or coarse flour.

Dating evidence shows the second mill was built in the middle of the ninth century and was destroyed by fire. It is possible the mill was torched during a Viking raid but an accidental fire is just as likely. Dust and friction make a highly flammable combination. The earlier mill on the site may have been operational a century earlier. Correspondence between Charlemagne and Offa mentions 'black stones', almost certainly a reference to a type of Rhineland lava rock

highly prized in Anglo-Saxon England for making grindstones.

The last of a series of 15 surviving royal charters issued from Tamworth is dated 857 and signed by King Burgred. In 874-5 a Danish army plundered deep into Mercia. Royal Tamworth, a tempting prize, was looted and burned to the ground. Burgred fled to Rome and never returned.

With a pragmatic mix of armed resistance and bribery, Alfred, King of the West Saxons maintained control of Wessex and part of south-west Mercia. The rest of England, broadly all the land north and east of Watling Street, came under Danish rule and became known as the Danelaw. For forty years Tamworth lay in no-man's land, the royal buildings reduced to blackened ruins on a lawless frontier.

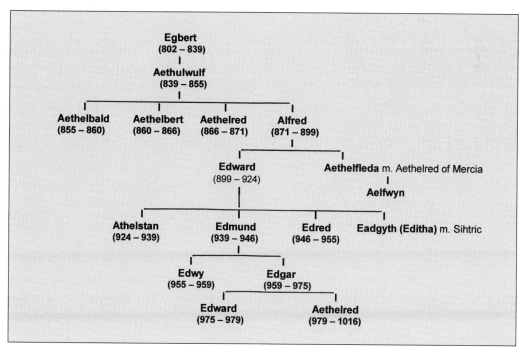

11 *The Royal House of Wessex (802-1016). Alfred, King of Wessex from 871, led Saxon resistance to Danish invaders. He put his daughter Aethelfleda in charge of Mercia. She made Tamworth, strategically placed on the frontier of the Danelaw, her base.*

Royal Burh: the Lady of the Mercians and King Athelstan

Alfred began a process of introducing centralised government, corralling the established hundred hide units into shire counties with defined boundaries. Each hundred was responsible for supplying and manning the garrison of a burh or fortified town at its centre. The military logic was based on the calculation that if each hide supplied one man that would ensure four men were available to defend every pole, or five and a half yards, of the town walls. Alfred delegated responsibility for Mercia to his daughter Aethelfleda and her husband Aethelred. When Aethelred died Aethelfleda took sole charge. As the site of a former royal residence now bordering enemy-held territory, Tamworth was significant both symbolically and strategically. In 913, Aethelfleda made Tamworth her base and began extending the chain of burhs envisaged by her father. An area of approximately fifty acres formed the heart of a new town, with the Tame and the Anker marking the southern boundary. On the other three sides a V-shaped ditch, bridged by a timber walkway at entrance points, surrounded a stepped turf and stone rampart topped by a palisade. Superimposed on a modern map of the town, the defences run from the Tame near Lady Bridge northwards behind Silver Street and Orchard Street. They turn east just before Hospital Street, where bolstered foundations discovered during excavation work point to a platform tower at the corner, and extending to the junction of Albert Road and Marmion Street. Another bastion was indicated at the angle where the ramparts return south along the line of Mill Lane to the Anker.

It was probably during the reconstruction of 913 that the division of Tamworth between two adjacent one hundred hide units, Offlow Hundred and Hemlingford Hundred, took place. A zigzag boundary neatly partitioned the borough into two, one side in Staffordshire and the other in Warwickshire. Possibly it was a diplomatic solution to avoid border problems, but a more convincing suggestion is that shared responsibility between two separately administered hundreds was necessary to ensure that sufficient manpower was available to guard the full extent of the town's defences.

For the farmers and craftspeople of the area the division between Saxon England and the Danelaw was not absolute. Many Saxons lived peacefully under Danish administration, just as a number of Danes settled in Saxon Mercia. Layout of the town within the burh follows a grid pattern model adopted in other new Saxon burhs of the time, for example at Winchester, and is a sign of active planning. Outside the defences an irregular skein of streets between Gungate and Aldergate, both thoroughfares containing the Danish 'gate' suffix, meaning street, appears to have grown piecemeal.

The *Anglo-Saxon Chronicle* credits Aethelfleda with building a castle at Tamworth. It is possible the present castle mound includes an earlier earthwork but the reference is much more likely to reflect the fortifying of the town, not a castle in the sense we would understand such a structure. In any case, Aethelfleda was working at speed. Tamworth's defences took only a matter of weeks to complete before Aethelfleda moved on to repeat the process at Stafford.

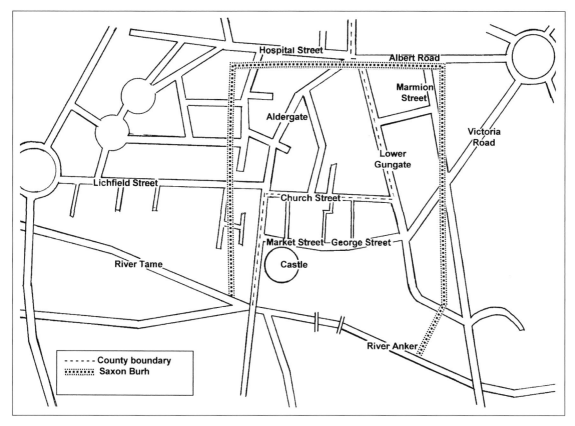

12 *The Anglo-Saxon borough. The defences of 913 enclosed an area of approximately fifty acres. A V-shaped ditch surrounded ramparts of stone and turf surmounted by a palisade, with the rivers forming a southern barrier. It is possible that the zigzag boundary dividing the borough between Staffordshire and Warwickshire has its origins in a shared responsibility for manning the walls.*

Over the next six years the formidable 'Lady of the Mercians' waged an unrelenting and successful campaign to prise the land from Viking grip. It was not just the Danes she had to face. Various Welsh tribal chieftains recognised an ideal opportunity to raid Saxon territory. Taking the battle to the enemy, Aethelfleda drove Welsh and Danes alike back to the Danelaw stronghold of Derby where she inflicted a crushing defeat and captured the town. Witnessing Aethelfleda's tactical skill and inspired leadership was Athelstan, Alfred's favourite though possibly illegitimate grandson. The

warrior lady acted as both role model and tutor to her young nephew.

Aethelfleda died at Tamworth in 918. Her brother, King Edward, swept aside local opposition and Aethelfleda's daughter Aelfwyn, to assume control of Mercia. After Edward's death in 924, the Saxon nobles gathered at Tamworth for a great council and named Athelstan 'King of all the English'. Athelstan continued where his aunt had left off. On the back of decisive military success against the Danish armies, he was able to dictate conditions for a peace deal with Northumbria's Hiberno-Norse king, Sihtric

Caoch. Under the terms of this treaty Sihtric agreed to accept baptism into the Christian faith and to marry one of Athelstan's sisters. Both marriage and conversion turned out to be brief. Sihtric soon abandoned his bride and his new religion. Sihtric's Saxon wife has been identified as Editha, patron saint of the parish church, and the claim is made that after being deserted she retired to a life of chastity and prayer with the nuns of Polesworth Abbey. In fact there is no record of the name of Sihtric's bride. Athelstan did have sisters, including one called Eadgyth (Edith), but she married Emperor Otto, cementing a continental alliance with the Saxon royal house. The elusive St Editha is much more likely to have been the daughter of King Egbert, who founded Polesworth Abbey in 827 and appointed his daughter the first abbess.

What Athelstan failed to achieve by negotiation and diplomacy he proceeded to gain by force of arms, beginning with the annexation of Northumbria. He later inflicted a crushing defeat on a combined force of Danes, British and Scots led by Anlaf, Sihtric's son from an earlier marriage and claimant to the throne of Northumbria.

Athelstan's dominance allowed a period of relative stability in these turbulent times, a chance to focus on administrative matters. Coins, out of circulation after the currency ceased to be backed by Rome, were gradually reintroduced from around 700. Offa issued a series of silver pennies from the mint he acquired at Canterbury, creating a standard rate of 12 pence to one shilling and 240 pence to one pound that lasted until decimalisation in 1971. Coins bearing the king's name and likeness were the only form of currency available. Athelstan was well aware of the power that control of it conferred both economically and symbolically. He laid down precise laws to ensure a crown monopoly, the king alone supplying the dies from which coins were struck. To maintain confidence and trust in the coinage 'moneyers' were subject to strict quality control and severe penalties were prescribed for failure to comply. Any moneyer caught betraying his responsibilities risked having a hand cut off and nailed above his workshop door. It is during Athelstan's reign that coins from a mint at Tamworth begin to appear, some bearing the name of

13 *Statue of Aethelfleda and Athelstan, the Lady of the Mercians with her nephew, erected in the Castle Grounds in 1913 to commemorate the millennium of the borough fortifications. It was designed by local stonemason Henry Mitchell and sculpted by Edward Bramwell, who studied art in the town.*

14 *The Abbey Church of St Editha, Polesworth (c.1900). King Egbert of Mercia founded Polesworth Abbey, dedicated to the Blessed Virgin Mary, in 872. Egbert's daughter Editha was the first abbess of the Benedictine Nunnery and is probably St Editha, patron saint of Tamworth church.*

a local moneyer called Manna. Of those silver pennies definitely attributable to the mint at Tamworth the best preserved are now in Scandinavian museum collections, presumably part of the huge sums of tribute known as Danegeld paid in later years in a vain attempt to buy off successive waves of invading Vikings.

Soon after Athelstan's death in 939, Anlaf exacted revenge, striking hard and deep into Saxon territory. Tamworth paid the price of its importance. Once again the town suffered systematic devastation. It was primarily a punitive foray. Retribution and booty was the aim rather than occupation. Athelstan's half brothers, Edred and Edmund, soon reclaimed possession. Tamworth survived but its pre-eminence as a royal base was over.

Town, Trade and the End of the Anglo-Saxon Era

What made Anglo-Saxon Tamworth a 'town'? It was not size that mattered. Primarily it was about safety and control. For their own protection, and to ensure operations were supervised, mints were only

15 *Silver penny of King Offa. Coins bearing the
king's name and likeness were the only form of mass
media in the Dark Ages. Offa issued a series of silver
pennies and created a standard rate of 12 pence to one
shilling and 240 pence to one pound that lasted until
decimalisation in 1971.*

allowed at fortified sites. For the same
reasons trade was restricted to towns where
the coinage fuelled commercial activity. Port-
reeves were appointed to collect tax on
merchandise. They also exercised basic
consumer protection, ensuring standards
were met for weights and measures and that
there was adherence to legal trading times.
As a town, Tamworth held an assembly
where its freemen met to decide matters of
community interest and over which the port-
reeve presided.

A large village might have a priest, a miller
and perhaps a smith but most inhabitants
would be involved in farming, working their
own and their lord's land. In towns a system
of burgage tenure associated with borough
status evolved to become the mainspring of
local economic development. Arrangements
allowed strips of land with a narrow street
frontage to be rented for commercial
purposes and attracted merchants and craft
specialists to set up businesses. In return for
renting plots, the 'burgesses', as they were
known, acquired certain freedoms and
privileges. Importantly, these included
freedom from feudal obligations and rights
of inheritance. Subject to certain conditions,
burgage holdings could be sold or handed
down. Our Saturday market, with its
temporary, open-air stalls and traders
shouting their wares, is a direct descendant
of the first markets held in the Anglo-Saxon
town.

Two

CONQUEST AND CASTLE:
DOMESDAY AND THE MARMIONS

After their narrow but decisive victory at the Battle of Hastings the Norman army pushed rapidly north. Saxon England was a rich prize. Subjugation of its people was brutal, ruthless and thorough. William of Normandy began progressively to parcel out the land between himself and his nobles. When the occupying forces arrived at Tamworth the local population was put to work. Ramparts were refurbished and a further ditch and substantial bank added around the outside of the existing defences. Visible signs of an entrenchment, known as both the 'King's Ditch' and confusingly 'Offa's Dyke', remained until recently. Sections uncovered during building and redevelopment work in the town centre show signs of both Saxon earthworks and later additions.

To make room for the great castle mound or motte, the south-western corner of Aethelfleda's burh was cleared. The mound was constructed of earth and stone in alternate layers, compacted to prevent erosion. It measures 80m. across at its base and rises steeply to a plateau, where initially a wooden tower and palisade were erected and a deep well was dug. Immediately below the mound an open area or bailey was enclosed with a ditch and timber stockade to contain stables and barrack buildings. This motte and bailey design is typically Norman, not pretty, but functional and effective. The castle dominated the town and commanded the approach from Watling Street. A gatehouse probably guarded the river crossing.

By 1070 or very soon after, the castle was under the control of Robert le Despencer, a royal steward. Ownership of the town remained with King William. Robert was given the castle 'grounds' or 'liberty' and associated land outside the borough. His possessions included Castle Orchard (between modern Orchard Street and Aldergate), land between the River Tame and Kettlebrook that later became the castle park, and Polesworth, site of the Saxon abbey. Action to rebuild St Editha's church on a grander scale probably began in the early days of the Norman takeover but the Benedictine nuns of Polesworth were expelled and the abbey confiscated.

Domesday Tamworth

There is a question mark over the exact date of Domesday Book. Popularly supposed to have been carried out in 1086, a case can be made for a survey completed in 1088-9, in the reign of William Rufus. Intended as a basis for resolving disputes over land rights and to assess tax liabilities,

16   *Tamworth Castle, a sandstone shell-keep on an artificial mound or 'motte', typical of Norman strongholds, described by the historian Leland in 1541 as 'a great round towre of stone'.*

there was no appeal against its findings. Royal commissioners armed with a checklist of questions visited every shire. The fiscal inventory they produced builds on the Saxon feudal system of hides and hundreds already in place. In a survey that is generally comprehensive elsewhere, Tamworth is unaccountably missing. Twenty-two burgesses of the town do appear but only in a passing reference and attached to the manors of Coleshill, Drayton Bassett and Wigginton. Shire division between Staffordshire and Warwickshire along the centre of Gungate, Church Street, Silver Street and Holloway may have confused the commissioners. Were records for Tamworth kept separately, pending a decision from a higher authority on where they should be included, and subsequently forgotten or mislaid?

The Marmions

Roger Marmion, married to Robert le Despencer's niece, inherited the castle around 1095. The Marmions were lords of Fontenay-le-Marmion in Normandy, land they held in return for service as the king's champion. Initially this may have meant actively representing the royal colours against rivals at jousting tourneys and in the rather barbarous mêlées relished as entertainment by the Norman nobles. In later times it became more of a nominal role, requiring the holder of the post to issue a ceremonial challenge at coronation services to any opposed to the crowning of the new monarch.

Men who rule by force rather than consent and live in the midst of their enemies need heavyweight protection. Over the next two centuries successive Marmion lords rebuilt their castle in sandstone, beginning with the shell-keep and ending with a gatehouse at the Market Street entrance. The shell-keep is a roughly five-sided wall against

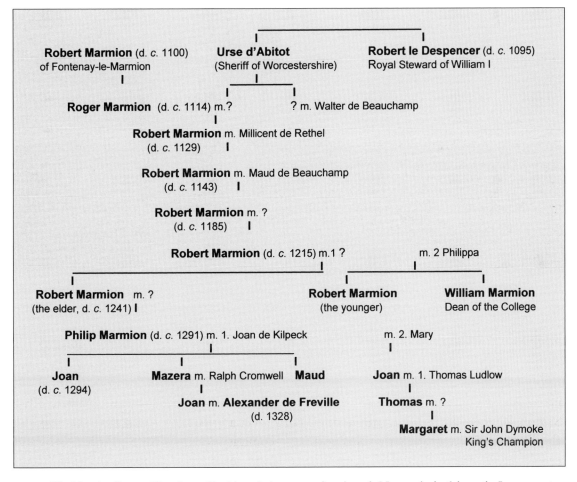

17 *The Marmion Barons. There is considerable confusion surrounding the early Norman lords of the castle. Some accounts treat Robert Marmion of Fontenay-le-Marmion and Robert le Despencer as the same person but it seems most likely that Roger Marmion inherited after marrying the royal steward's niece, a daughter of Urse d'Abitot.*

18   *Castle 'dungeon'. A square windowless room at the base of the tower set into the walls of the shell-keep is popularly known as the dungeon but was probably used primarily as a storeroom.*

which the inner domestic buildings lean, integrating a massively solid square tower with walls 4.3m. thick. A windowless room at the base of the tower has been known as the dungeon but was probably intended primarily as a storeroom. A watch over the surrounding countryside could be kept from the battlements and from strategically placed loopholes reached by passageways built into the keep wall.

Fragments of what was once a three-storey gatehouse remain at the foot of the curtain wall. Entry was via a wooden causeway crossing a dry moat. A drawbridge, operated by a winch in the upper storey of the gatehouse, controlled access, with a

portcullis for extra security. Arrow slits in the basement allowed archers to guard the moat.

A stretch of distinctive and exceptionally fine herringbone masonry, vestiges of the inner bailey bulwark built by the Marmions, still stands. Running along the top of the wall today is a footpath leading from the castle entrance to the ruins of the former gatehouse. With some interruptions, when the Marmions chose to put their name to temporarily losing causes, the castle remained in the family for eight generations.

Polesworth Abbey was returned to the nuns in 1139, according to legend after a vision of St Editha appeared one night to berate the then baron for continuing to deny the nuns their rights. Threatening him with damnation and hitting him over the head with her crozier, St Editha caused a wound she said would never heal unless the land was returned. The deed of Robert Marmion's subsequent bequest is addressed to 'the prelates and ministers of the Holy Church of God as well present as to come and especially to Henry II, King of the English and to Theobald, Archbishop of Canterbury and to Walter, Bishop of Chester'. It is made 'for my salvation and for the soul of my father and of my mother and sister and all my ancestors' and confirms his gift of 'all of the vill of Polisworda and Wavertune'. The one right he reserves for himself and his heirs is to hunt across the land, but even then the grant allows the nuns access to the surrounding woods for pannage, pasture and firewood.

Robert Marmion actively supported King Stephen in his fight with Empress Matilda, daughter of Henry I, for the throne of

19   *View from the castle battlements, looking north from the ramparts. Loopholes tactically placed at the end of passageways in the keep wall enabled a watch to be kept over the surrounding town and countryside.*

20   *Medieval gatehouse. Remains of a three-storey late 13th-century gatehouse at the Market Street entrance to the Castle Grounds. A drawbridge controlled access across a dry moat that was guarded by archers in the basement.*

21   *Herringbone masonry, inner bailey wall. A stretch of distinctive and well-preserved herringbone masonry is all that now remains of the inner bailey or curtain wall. The footpath leading to the castle entrance runs along the top.*

22 *'Haunted' bedroom. The middle room of the castle's Norman tower was used as a solar or private chamber adjoining the first-floor hall, and is, according to legend, the scene of St Editha's appearance to Robert Marmion in 1139.*

England. In the struggle, the castle fell to Matilda's forces and was occupied on her behalf by Sir William de Beauchamp. Meanwhile, in France, Matilda's husband Geoffrey of Anjou captured and destroyed the Marmions' ancestral castle at Fontenay.

Robert Marmion met an undignified end on the battlefield in 1143, thrown when his horse slipped in one of his own defensive ditches and summarily despatched where he lay. His body was taken for burial to Polesworth Abbey but the nuns refused him a place of honour, allocating instead a corner of the abbey orchard.

His son Robert regained the castle soon after Stephen finally prevailed over his cousin, ending 'the anarchy' and restoring a

semblance of peace to the land in 1148. He was succeeded in turn by his son, also Robert, a knight-justiciary. Sir Robert served in the army and on the King's Bench as a travelling justice for the Midlands under a newly introduced legal system. Technically, only freemen had recourse to the royal courts. In practice the king's justice was available to anyone who had the means to pay.

Sir Robert married twice and had three sons. The two oldest were both called Robert, not as unusual as it might sound if your wish was to ensure that a family name survived in an age of high mortality rates. Robert the elder soldiered in France against King John, a clash that ended with John losing his French territories in Brittany,

Hen. 2.

23 *Grant of Polesworth Abbey to the nuns. Robert Marmion's confirmation of the return of Polesworth Abbey to the nuns was allegedly prompted by the appearance of St Editha one night threatening the baron with eternal damnation if he failed to comply.*

Maine, Anjou and, the bitterest blow of all, Normandy. Marmion opposition to John, in particular Sir Robert's support for the reforms demanded of the crown by a rebellious group of powerful barons, led to the castle being taken by Thomas de Erdington, John's chamberlain and sheriff of Shropshire. At Runnymede, the barons forced John to accept their demands for constitutional constraints on royal power contained in Magna Carta. In the aftermath a vengeful King John threatened Tamworth Castle with destruction but no action was taken. The castle survived. After Sir Robert's death, in 1215, Robert the younger paid £500 to be allowed to reclaim tenancy of the castle. The youngest brother, William, brokered

reconciliation for Robert the elder, either directly with King John shortly before his death or with William Marshal on behalf of the boy who succeeded as Henry III. Robert senior's return to claim his inheritance triggered sibling rivalry. Matters simmered until an agreement was reached by which Robert junior acquired the family estates in Lincolnshire and elsewhere and his mother received a settlement agreed at a specially commissioned hearing. In 1257, William Marmion became the first recorded Dean of the College.

The town remained crown property until 1238, when Henry III exchanged the Staffordshire half of the town for land in Cheshire and Henry de Hastings became the

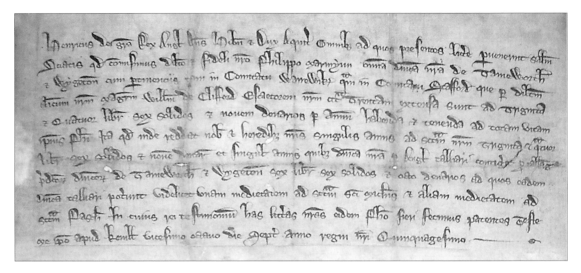

24 *Deed of Henry III, 1266. King Henry assigned the manors of Wigginton and Tamworth to Philip Marmion for life as a reward for support during the Barons' Revolt.*

25 *Spital Chapel, 1850. Originally planned by Philip Marmion as a chantry chapel for prayers to be said for his soul and those of his family, it survived until the Reformation as a place of rest for travellers and as an infirmary. The name is a contraction of 'hospital'.*

new lord of the manor. Robert the elder died in 1241. His son, Philip Marmion, appears to have lived pretty much as he pleased, showing little regard for others. He claimed to hunt only on his own land at Middleton but records of the King's Court Eyre, the special forest courts that had jurisdiction over Cannock and Kinver, contain repeated allegations of poaching in the royal forests and on Sutton Chase. He was not a good neighbour. Quarrels and disputes with Henry de Hastings of Wigginton and Ralph Bassett, lord of the manor of Drayton, led to bad feeling. In the Barons' Revolt, led by Simon de Montfort, Earl of Leicester, the local lords took opposing sides. Hastings and Bassett supported de Montfort. Marmion declared for the King and ran the rebel blockade at Kenilworth Castle to supply the besieged royal garrison. Philip Marmion probably fought beside Henry at Evesham, the final battle of the conflict in 1265, at which both de Montfort and Bassett were killed. His reward was to be granted the manor of Wigginton and both the Staffordshire and Warwickshire sides of the town for life.

Pursuing an agenda aimed at strengthening a future claim on the estates by his heirs, Philip Marmion established a chantry chapel in Wigginton parish dedicated to St James, where prayers would be said for his soul and for those of his family. His intention was to bring in a group of Premonstratensian canons, a religious group that worked actively in local communities. A temporary master and brothers were installed but Marmion was running short of funds. Proper endowment proved difficult to arrange and the religious house originally planned was never

26 *Spital Chapel, interior. Fortnightly communion services are still held in the simple surroundings of the restored chapel linked to St Leonard's church, Wigginton. Inside, nave and chancel together measure just 11 metres in length.*

27 *The Marmion Stone, sometimes called the 'cross and dial', was probably the base of a wayside cross or statue of the Virgin Mary that once stood on Lady Bridge. Any inscriptions have long since weathered away but records claim it once bore the Bassett arms and religious dedications.*

established. Spital Chapel, as it became known, survived to serve as a place where travellers could rest and pray, and possibly as an infirmary.

Philip Marmion had four daughters from two marriages and an illegitimate son, Robert. In 1285, lordship of the Staffordshire borough and the manor of Wigginton had been restored to Hastings' descendants by royal command. When Philip died in 1291, ownership of the Warwickshire part of the town returned to the crown. Tenancy of the castle passed in quick succession to Philip's eldest daughter Joan, then to his second daughter Mazera, and in 1294 to Mazera's daughter Joan and her husband, Alexander de Freville. Another Joan, Philip's youngest daughter and the only child of his second marriage, inherited Scrivelsby, a manor held by the Marmions in Lincolnshire.

A large masonry block known as the 'Marmion Stone' or 'cross and dial' stands outside the castle keep. It is thought to be a pedestal that once held a statue or wayside cross. Such symbols frequently marked boundaries or were placed at river crossings as a focus for travellers' prayers. Any inscription the stone once bore has long since eroded away. Early accounts claim the block bore the Bassett arms, the initials IHS (for Jesus) and a dedication to the Virgin Mary. It is quite likely to have stood on Lady Bridge (originally 'the bridge of St Mary' or 'Our Lady'). Reference to a bridge rather than a ford across the Tame at the southern entrance to the town occurs right at the end of the Marmion era, in 1294. Until 1872, the Marmion Stone had for many years been built into the west parapet of Lady Bridge.

The Norman Town

From Domesday Book it is clear that the countryside around Tamworth at the time of the Conquest was well wooded. Saxon nobles enjoyed the chase but the Normans hunted with passion. Herds of fallow deer were imported. Woodland was set aside where harsh forest laws protected the animals and even the king's barons needed licence to take game or fell trees. When Domesday was compiled, Cannock Chase had already been designated a royal forest, its boundaries then extending to the River Tame. This made Tamworth an attractive place to visit. Henry I, Henry II, with his then chancellor Thomas Becket; and Henry III all came to stay here, probably taking advantage of Marmion hospitality at the castle.

Reforms curbing the power of the king led to national councils, the forerunners of our modern parliament, being summoned to meet in London. Under Simon de Montfort, Tamworth was ignored perhaps because of Marmion opposition to the Earl of Leicester's cause. But in 1275 Edward I invited two burgesses of the town to attend an assembly.

In the 12th and 13th centuries this was a land divided. The language of the court and administration was French. Many of the Norman barons still owned estates in Normandy, and their sons were sent for education to religious houses in France. A branch of the Marmion family continued to live in the shadow of the ruined castle at Fontenay. For most ordinary townspeople, though, while the Marmions of Tamworth and their lordly neighbours played their part in the events that shaped history, life was about coping with the everyday struggle to survive.

28 *Tamworth Castle and Castle Mill. In the 13th century, townspeople were expected to bring all their grain to be ground into flour at the Castle Mill. When this painting was first published the mill complex was being used for spinning cotton.*

Although there was no confirmatory royal charter, the town's ancient rights to operate as a borough and to hold markets were never disputed. Separate markets were held on each side of the town. The Warwickshire stalls were probably always set up in and around Market Street. Staffordshire's market was held at the corner of Church Street, Colehill and Gungate. Colehill was formerly called Cross Street and a stone cross is recorded here in 1293 at the junction with Church Street. It was common practice in medieval times to erect a cross where markets were held to remind traders of

their Christian duty to conduct business honestly. Stocks and a pillory were positioned nearby as a reminder of the earthly consequences of being caught serving customers short measure or selling food unfit for consumption. In 1294, Nicholas Alcus was found guilty of selling underweight loaves. It was not his first offence and, under an early example of the 'three strikes and they throw the book at you' principle, he was sentenced to a whipping at the pillory.

Most of Tamworth's inhabitants were classed as villeins, a labouring peasantry

29 *Silver pennies from the Tamworth Mint struck by Bruninc. Coins by Bruninc and another moneyer called Colinc span the transition from Saxon to Norman rule. Coins of Edward the Confessor and William I were part of a hoard discovered during building work in Marmion Street in 1877.*

cultivating land in return for owing service to the lord of the manor. Economically and legally they were tied to the manorial system. As temporary lord of both the Warwickshire and Staffordshire parts of the borough from 1265-85, Philip Marmion was in a dominant position. Inhabitants were expected to bring all their grain for grinding at the Castle Mill, standing in the Castle Grounds near the confluence of the Tame and Anker. Milling has always been contentious. A share of the flour was kept by the mill as payment, but because it is impossible to estimate with any accuracy how much flour can be expected from any given quantity of corn the door is open to sharp practice and suspicion. In a move guaranteed to annoy his belligerent neighbour, Ralph Bassett of Drayton invited the tenants of Tamworth to use his Lady Mill, beside the River Tame near Bitterscote. A furious Philip Marmion recruited a rag-tag force of Welsh roughs to break into Bassett's mill and seize the flour. Considerable damage

was caused in the affray that followed and both Marmion and Bassett faced charges. The two noble lords were censured for bringing in unsavoury mercenary 'muscle' and bound over to keep the peace.

A mint continued to operate into the middle of the 12th century. In 1877, a 294-coin hoard from the time of William I and William Rufus was discovered during building work in Marmion Street. Thirty-three of the coins had been struck here. An interesting degree of continuity at the local mint is implied by the names of the same two moneyers, Bruninc and Colinc, appearing on coins struck for Edward the Confessor before the Conquest and on those produced for the new Norman kings.

Domesday Book records burgesses from Tamworth engaged in farming activity on land belonging to nearby manors. As far as we know, there were no open fields attached to the borough itself, but householders had the right to pasture horses and cattle on one of two areas of common moor depending on which side of the borough they lived. Staffordshire Moor may originally have been part of Wigginton, and Warwickshire Moor, or the Port Moor as it was sometimes known, attached to Bolehall Manor. We can be reasonably certain this land would have been in communal use for pasturing livestock under the pre-Conquest system of collective farming.

The population was increasing but still small, perhaps around one hundred and fifty families. Everyone knew everyone else in the community. Surnames were descriptive, often reflecting an individual's trade, as in 'Cooper', 'Brewster' or 'Skinner', or where they lived, as in 'Gumpigate' (Gungate), 'Bradford' (after the 'Broad Ford' that gave access over the Tame between Lichfield Street and Lady Meadow) and 'at the cross' (presumably the market cross).

Norman bailiffs were appointed to replace port-reeves in Saxon boroughs unless a fixed levy, known as fee farm rent, was paid annually. Electing officers locally ensured a degree of independence and control over affairs, and the burgesses of the town were prepared to pay for this privilege via the King's Court held at Wigginton. Tamworth under the Normans was not prosperous. With something of an economic boom underway in the country at large there was increasing competition. New markets developed nearby in Abbots Bromley, Burton upon Trent, Lichfield and Wolverhampton, all vying for custom in small overlapping catchment areas constrained by how far individuals could travel in daylight on poor roads. During the 12th century there were occasions when payment of fee farm rent

was reduced or excused altogether, reflecting conditions of poverty in the town going beyond a merely depressed state of trade. In 1222, a county report refers to the 'villata' of Tamworth rather than the town or borough.

The Staffordshire and Warwickshire sides of Tamworth were independent but, in effect, worked together co-operatively. Both elected their own bailiffs and officials, usually appointed to serve for a fixed term of twelve months. The bailiff's administrative duties including presiding at the town courts and ensuring fines and tolls were collected. Fee farm rent was paid out of court profits. A portmanmoot court met every three weeks to deal with property disputes, matters of probate, debt and infringements of trading regulations. Twice a year, in spring and autumn, a leet court, or court of view of frankpledge, met to elect town officials, enact bylaws and ensure that all those eligible were members of a tithing, or frankpledge as the groups became known under Norman rule. Separate courts for each side of the town met on the same day and a record of proceedings was entered on a single court roll. Decisions were based as much on custom and precedent as on statute law. Much of what went on was regarded as 'town secrets' and not written down. Burgesses could be, and on occasion were, expelled from their tithing for refusing to maintain confidentiality, effectively removing their right to conduct business in the town.

There were two keys to a single common chest, probably lodged for safety in St Editha's church, where the court proceeds from fines and tolls were kept. A bailiff for Warwickshire held one key, his Staffordshire counterpart a second. Witnesses representing

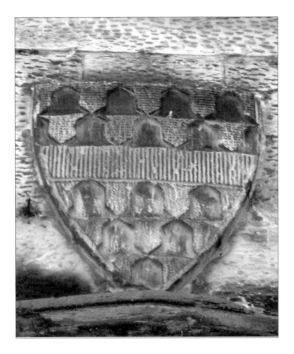

30 *Weathered shield of the Marmion coat-of-arms above the Holloway Lodge entrance to the Castle Grounds.*

each side of the borough were required to be present if the chest were opened. The role of bailiff was part mayor, part magistrate and part tax collector, a powerful position but not above the law. In 1204, the Tamworth bailiffs were summoned to appear before the Staffordshire County Assizes accused of charging visiting traders illegal and unfair tolls.

Disputes over access were a frequent occurrence. The monks of Merevale Abbey, founded by Robert de Ferrers in the middle of the 12th century, owned an area in the Warwickshire half of the town beside the River Anker, known as Segorisgate. Problems were caused when the path to the river, where the townspeople had fishing rights and customarily fetched water, was blocked. Philip Marmion's attempts to ride roughshod over the burgesses after he was granted temporary lordship of both the Staffordshire and Warwickshire sides of the borough led to an outcry about infringement of common rights, seizure of land and obstruction of the bailiffs. A commission set up in 1275 to investigate complaints ruled in favour of the townspeople. The increasingly independent inhabitants of the borough had refused to be intimidated. Even so, by the time of his death Philip Marmion had appropriated a strip of land belonging to the Warwickshire market place and incorporated it into the castle precincts.

Three

THE LATE MIDDLE AGES: LIFE, DEATH AND FIRE

Early 14th-century Tamworth is a growing town. Houses cluster alongside the roads on the outskirts of the borough. Outwalls Street (Otewallestrete), stretching beyond the town ditch, is first mentioned. Later it will become known as Lichfield Street. Sections of ditch are rented out for cultivation. Bole Bridge (Bollebrugge) across the River Anker (Oncur) is built to improve access into the town. Bridge wardens are appointed by the burgesses to be responsible for the maintenance of Bole Bridge and Lady Bridge. Bollebruggestrete (Bolebridge Street) and Bollenhull (Bonehill) appear in records for the first time. George Street is known as the Bullstake or Bullstake Street, named from the post that stands at the junction with Cross Street (Colleshull/Colehill). Before being slaughtered, skinned and butchered, bulls are baited by dogs, partly for the entertainment

31　*Old Bole Bridge (c.1870). The narrow 12-arched medieval bridge, replaced in 1878-9, was built with a dogleg to reduce resistance to the current. A bridge across the River Anker is first mentioned in 1316.*

32   *George Street (1912). In the Middle Ages bulls were tethered at the junction of George Street and Colehill to be baited before slaughter. Baiting was believed to improve the quality of the meat and was compulsory. Bull baiting remained a legal entertainment until 1835.*

spectacle it provides but also because the exercise is thought to improve the quality of the meat. Baiting is compulsory and butchers face a fine for killing an animal that has not been baited.

Land in the centre of town is at a premium. Unlike newer boroughs, of which more than three thousand received charters in the 13th century, there is no standard-size burgage plot. The most valuable land borders the market areas, where narrow-fronted, timber-hung houses of lathe and plaster stand tightly packed together. Jettied upper storeys make the most of confined space, projecting over the muddy roads and

alleys that thread through the town. Temporary stalls set up outside front doors during trading hours, indicated by the ringing of a market bell, further constrict the cramped streets. Selling goods outside the permitted times or without bringing them to market, a practice known as forestalling, was a punishable offence.

Houses are sparsely furnished: a couple of benches, a trestle table and a collection of rudimentary kitchen utensils, earthenware cooking pots and wooden bowls. At the rear of some dwellings, poultry and a few sheep are penned on long narrow strips of garden. Eggs, butter and cheese are produced for sale.

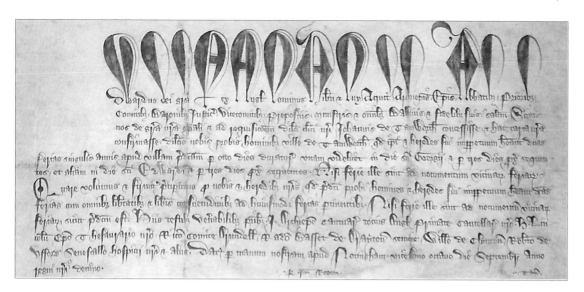

33 *Grant by Edward III, 1337; royal charter confirming the grant of two fairs annually, one in April and the other in October. Both events lasted for four days. With a variety of goods for sale and entertainment on offer, the fairs attracted extra business to the town.*

In 1317, Edward II granted permission for the town to charge an additional levy on goods brought into the town. This was a hypothecated tax, designed to raise funds to pay for the streets to be paved. Initially the royal licence was for just three years but it was renewed and tolls were re-imposed in following decades. After briefly renting the Warwickshire side of the town to Baldwin de Freville, King Edward accepted a higher bid from the burgesses and, in 1319, transferred the lease to the freemen of the town on a long-term basis. At the time, the latest baronial conspiracy, led by Thomas, Earl of Lancaster, was about to break out into open rebellion. Edward's action was consistent with a strategy aimed at pegging the power of the barons by strengthening an increasingly independent merchant class.

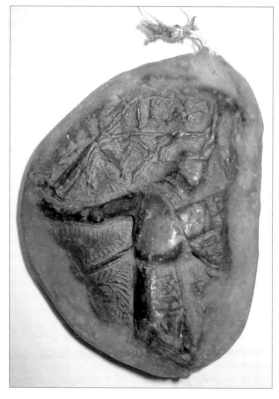

34 *Henry Jekes's seal. Jekes was Staffordshire bailiff in 1414 and 1427. Pendant seals were used to close and authenticate important documents. A length of silk cord, a linen tape, or vellum strip was threaded through the document. The ends were sealed in hot beeswax and the signatory's personal seal – often a likeness – impressed.*

35   *Church Street (1902), showing the Paregoric Shop, St George's Institute and indoor baths. In the Middle Ages this end of Church Street was known as the Butchery. By-laws were passed banning traders from throwing waste and entrails into the gutters outside their shops.*

By tradition, the town celebrated a 'Cherry Fair' held in July on the feast day of St Editha and organised by the church for its own benefit. In 1337, Edward III granted permission for two 'official' fairs to be held each year, one to take place in April and the other in October. Both events lasted for four days, with goods for sale and entertainment on offer. Tamworth's markets and fairs attracted extra business to the town and an additional court was also authorised. The court of piepowder (the name comes from the French *pied poudré*, literally 'dusty foot', a term used to describe a pedlar) was able to convene at short notice in order to deal speedily with cases involving visitors who were only in town for a few days.

Local courts became gradually more constitutional. Jurors were sworn in to approve bylaws. Each side of the borough appointed two bailiffs and two tasters and, beneath those officials, a growing team of executives: an under-bailiff whose job was to seize goods ordered by the court; a constable; and, by the middle of the 15th century, a chamberlain to handle the fines and tolls collected by the courts. Proceedings recorded in the court leet rolls offer a vivid insight into life in Tamworth in the high Middle Ages. Regulations restricted the washing of tripe to a section of the river downstream of the town at Lady Bridge where the current would carry the resulting residue away to become someone else's problem. An area at the Gungate (Gumpigate) end of what is now Church Street was known as the Butchery. In an attempt to ensure traders in the area kept the gutters outside their premises clear an order was enacted forbidding the disposal of entrails in the street.

Waste was frequently simply thrown out into the thoroughfares or dumped in the river. In common with other medieval towns, pigs were often allowed to scavenge as mobile street cleaners. Left to roam, such animals could develop hooligan tendencies. In 1423, a regulation was passed in the court leet making owners liable to a fine if animals were loose after nightfall. The town collectively employed a swineherd, an oxherd and a shepherd to keep watch on animals grazing communal pasture. Domestic animals caught wandering were taken to the pinfold on Bolebridge Street and owners paid a fine to release their livestock. Dogs too were subject to a curfew and not allowed out at night unless accompanied by their owners.

A watch is recorded in Tamworth for the first time in the early years of the 14th century. The Town Watch patrolled the streets and a separate Church Watch guarded St Editha's church. Manning the watch was a communal exercise organised by the bailiffs. Everyone was expected to take a turn or to field a fit substitute. Penalties were imposed on those not performing their duty when required or failing to turn out in support of the hue and cry if the alarm were raised. The watch

operated from dusk until dawn and anyone caught wandering abroad in the small hours was liable to arrest. Watch members themselves were subject to control. A local bylaw banning those on duty from hanging about listening at shuttered windows, and backed by the threat of a hefty fine, reflects fears about membership of the watch being a licence to snoop. In a tightly knit community, gossiping was frowned upon. Those found guilty of dealing in scuttlebutt faced the shame of the cucking stool, a chair into which scandalmongers were tied and put on public display outside their own front door.

Petty infringement of trading regulations might lead to the stocks or pillory and to forfeiture of goods. If imprisonment were

36 *Tamworth pig. A primitive breed introduced into this country, possibly from Spain and some claim by Sir Robert Peel, towards the end of the 18th century. 'Sandies' or 'sandybacks', with their long snouts, heavy forequarters and pricked ears, closely resemble the old English forest pigs once kept semi-wild and fattened in autumn on beech mast and acorns.*

37 *Interior of a dovecote. Pigeons were once an important source of fresh protein in the winter months. Birds were kept in specially constructed dovecotes, the inside a honeycomb of nesting holes reached by a ladder.*

an option, it does not seem to have been one much exercised. For theft and worse crimes a gallows, the ultimate status symbol of a town's importance, stood on the parish boundary at the northern approach to the town near the junction of the Ashby, Comberford and Wigginton roads. Here the bodies of miscreants were left on display, a grim warning to those travelling into the town that any misdemeanours would be severely punished.

For most people life was squalid and unhealthy. Disease was rife and chronic conditions such as rheumatism and arthritis commonplace. Medical care hinged on herbal remedies and the power of prayer. Diet for the poorest was meagre. Black bread, vegetable stew and weak beer were the mainstays. Bread was a major part of the diet for all classes and its supply subject to regulation and price control by the courts. In 1428 a bylaw was approved stipulating 'that if the town be without bread … each baker pay eight pence, half to the bailiffs and half to the common chest'. Brewing, often a part-time occupation of individuals selling the household surplus, also had to stay within fixed price limits or face a hefty fine. Official tasters were appointed as a quality control measure to inspect and sample the goods on offer. In 1296 the court ordered 'that no one allow strange women to brew in his house under pain of half a mark'. The court's definition of a 'stranger' was anyone not a resident of the borough. In 1368, Welsh people were specifically singled out and banned from selling ale in Gungate.

Fish were netted or trapped in baskets from the rivers under licence. Monasteries and manor houses had their own ponds. Packhorse trains delivered goods not available locally, for example kippered herring, for sale in the market. Salt for preserving was an important commodity regularly brought in from the salt pans of Cheshire and Droitwich. A significant number of butchers is an indication that meat was readily available to those who could afford to buy. Of all the trades carried out in the borough, butchery was the only one whose practitioners were required to take an oath, sworn before the court, promising honourable business conduct. This was partly to try to ensure that meat sold was wholesome but also an attempt to guard against rustling, since cattle were unidentifiable once skinned and jointed. Individuals were consigned to the gallows in 1294 and 1332 for stealing livestock.

Hand in hand with butchery went tanning, another trade guaranteed to produce smells and unsavoury waste. Rabbits, introduced after the Norman Conquest and kept in warrens under baronial control, were a luxury item. The nobles supplemented their winter diet with pigeons housed in specially constructed dovecotes. Venison was beyond price.

Despite the watch, disaster struck in 1345 when a great fire ripped through the tinderbox of the town centre and gutted the parish church. Worse followed. Bubonic plague began in China and reached England in 1348. Over the next few decades as many as one in three of the population died. St James's Chapel was probably used primarily as an infirmary at this time and became known as the 'Spital', or Hospital Chapel. Because the Black Death had arrived on the south coast and then spread northwards, people believed it was carried on southerly winds. But it is, as they say, an ill wind that blows nobody any good. The long established manorial system depended on the availability of labour. For once, the urban wage-labourer found himself a marketable commodity and in a position to negotiate for his services. The plague hastened social changes that were to put an end to the feudal concept of tied labour. Desperate land-owners were prepared to outbid each other for services, and ten inhabitants of the borough were fined for not being available to help with harvesting the crops in 1366. It was a national problem and, in a bid to defy the laws of economics and restrict the movement of workers, the legislature passed the Statute of Labourers. It was backed up locally by a regulation of 1382 threatening

to fine any individual, deemed to owe service in the town, leaving for work elsewhere during the agricultural high seasons of spring or autumn.

Various levels of personal status had largely been reduced to just two, freemen and villeins. Now the days of villeinage were numbered. Towns, even poor towns, wanted to attract those ambitious to better themselves. It was a time of opportunity. Newcomers could qualify to join the free community of the town if they could prove residency, usually one year and a day, or by acquiring property, or, if they had relatives born in the town and could afford to, by paying the entrance fee required to be admitted into a tithing.

High Society

Edward II visited Tamworth and stayed as a guest of Alexander de Freville at the castle in 1325. Two years later, a fully armed Alexander, mounted astride a richly caparisoned warhorse, was part of the pageant at the coronation of Edward III. Alexander had been a soldier, serving under Edward I in the Anglo-Scottish wars a quarter of a century earlier. It was to be the last time that a lord of Tamworth Castle discharged his responsibility as king's champion. The Dymoke descendants of Philip Marmion's youngest daughter successfully claimed that the hereditary right to act as royal champion attached to the Lincolnshire manor of Scrivelsby. Sir John Dymoke took over for the crowning of Richard II and the family continued to officiate in the role until the post of champion was abandoned as an anachronism after the coronation of George IV, in 1820.

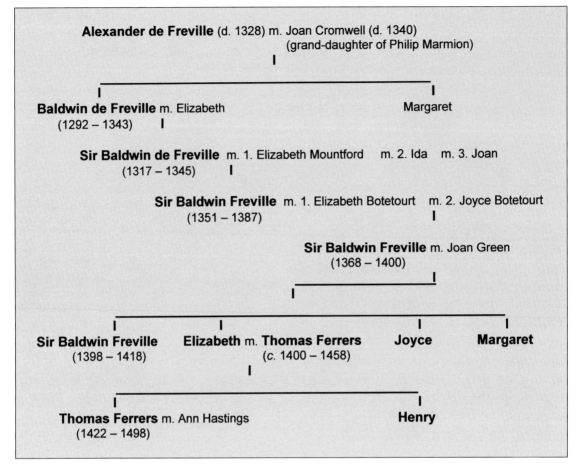

38 *The Freville family. Alexander de Freville was the last lord of Tamworth Castle to act as royal champion when he officiated at the coronation of Edward III in 1327. The role passed to the Dymoke descendants of Philip Marmion's youngest daughter, Margaret, until the post was abandoned as an anachronism following the coronation of George IV in 1820.*

Five generations of Frevilles followed Alexander at Tamworth Castle, all called Baldwin. When the last of the male line died, in 1418, title passed to his sister Elizabeth and her husband Thomas Ferrers of Groby, Leicestershire.

The Ferrers made Tamworth their main residence and rebuilt the Great Hall, or Banqueting Hall, as the centrepiece of life at the castle. Dendrochronology, a technique that compares tree ring samples against a national database, confirms that the oak

trees from which the roof beams are made were felled in 1437. A minstrels' gallery probably projected above screen doors at the southern end of the hall before the room was remodelled in 17th-century style, red brick replacing the original wattle and daub walls.

Edward IV was in the locality in 1468 and again in 1473. On one of these occasions the King is supposed to have met a tanner from Tamworth at Bassett's Pole and the story of their subsequent exchange was immortalised in a long ballad. Edward has become separated from his companions while hunting. Realising the man does not recognise him, Edward pretends to fall for a naive attempt to persuade him to exchange his spirited hunter for the tanner's broken down hack. Unable to handle the lively mount, the tanner is forced to buy back his old mare. At the end of the encounter, when Edward finally reveals his identity, the tanner fears for his life but he is rewarded instead by the gift of Plumpton Park.

When Thomas Ferrers inherited, in 1458, the dynastic struggle between the rival Yorkist and Lancastrian claims to the throne of England had begun. Edward IV's death triggered the last act in the Wars of the Roses. When Henry Tudor, Earl of Richmond landed at Milford Haven, Richard III was in northern England. The two men marched to meet their destiny at Bosworth Field in Warwickshire. On Thursday, 19 August 1485, three days before the battle, Henry's army set up camp for the night on Staffordshire Moor. It is here that Henry Tudor learns that Richard is at Leicester. In *Richard III* Shakespeare has Henry anticipating the coming clash with the words 'From Tamworth thither, is but one day's march.' Henry himself did not stay with his men that night and his absence gave rise to speculation. He may have slipped away secretly to visit his mother Margaret Beaufort, now married to her third husband Sir Thomas Stanley, and living at Elford Manor. The next morning Henry made a public reappearance to reassure his followers all was well before leaving again, this time to consult with Stanley himself at nearby Atherstone.

The Battle of Bosworth Field began as a finely balanced affair, with the Yorkist and Lancastrian forces evenly matched. Sir Thomas Ferrers and his eldest son John were among those lined up to fight alongside King Richard. Sir Thomas carried a sword inscribed 'He who loses me loses honour'. Stanley, with around five thousand men under his command, held a potentially pivotal role in the conflict. He was well aware that whichever side he supported was likely to be victorious. In the end Stanley

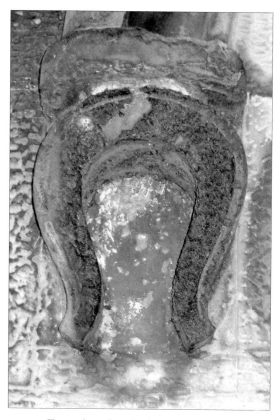

39 *Ferrers horseshoe, Holloway Lodge. The Ferrers took their surname from the small Normandy town of Ferriers, a centre of iron ore mining, and Old French for a farrier, adopting a horseshoe as their emblem. Decorative horseshoes added to the ends of dripstone moulding above the arch of Holloway Lodge are an allusion to the family arms.*

40   *The Great Hall, Tamworth Castle, built as the centrepiece of life at the castle by Thomas Ferrers. Dendrochronology samples from the oak ceiling beams confirm a felling date around 1437.*

sat on the fence, refusing to commit his forces until late in the day when the tide of the battle was becoming clear. He then pitched in decisively on behalf of the Lancastrians, personally handing Henry the crown amidst the carnage of the battlefield. Among the dead lay John Ferrers, Stanley's son-in-law. Stanley's reticence has been seen as a mercenary act prompted purely by pragmatic self-interest. But with a son held hostage by the Yorkists and his son-in-law and stepson fighting on opposing sides he was in an impossibly difficult situation. Perhaps it was the fall of John Ferrers that allowed him to join the fray with a clear conscience.

Four

CHURCH, COLLEGE AND THE REFORMATION

Evidence to support the existence of a Saxon church is tantalisingly sketchy, but collectively the indications make a convincing case. Tamworth was an important royal centre in the eighth century. Offa would never have chosen to spend Christmas here unless there was a church, probably a timber building, in which to celebrate mass. Consecrated sites enjoy such continuity of use that we can securely place this early church where St Editha's now stands, a natural high point in the centre of town and at the heart of the Anglo-Saxon borough. Destruction would have been a foregone conclusion when pagan Danish armies ransacked the town in 874-5 and again in the 940s.

Rebuilding the church in the middle of the 10th century after Anlaf's raid marked a gradual regeneration of Saxon Tamworth, possibly instigated by King Edgar around 963 and coincidental with Editha's canonisation. Dedication of the church to a Saxon saint implies foundation before the arrival of the Normans. The ghost of a Saxon crossing tower has been identified in the fabric above the chancel arches, suggesting the rebuilding was in stone. Roughly hewn masonry in lower parts of the south chancel wall may also date from this period. At approximately 60m., St Editha's is one of the longest parish churches

in the county. An uninterrupted string course projecting from ancient masonry points to an original stone building of a similar size.

41 *Early masonry, St Editha's church. Dedication to a Saxon saint suggests a church on the site before the Norman Conquest. Roughly hewn masonry in lower parts of the south chancel wall may date from the first stone church on the site.*

We are dealing with likelihood rather than hard evidence, but there are sufficient clues for us to conclude that there was a church here before the Norman Conquest and that it was a substantial structure.

Less certain is how St Editha's was organised. We know that there was a religious community in the town by late Saxon times. In his will, ratified by King Aethelred himself in 1004, high-ranking Mercian nobleman and local landowner Wulfric Spot confirms the return of an estate at Longdon 'to the community (*do Convetuni*) at Tamworth (*Tamwurthie*)'. Assuming St Editha's was originally a minster church, with priests serving an extensive parish, allows us to explain what happened to Wulfric's 'convent' (a loose enough term at the time and applied to a wide range of religious groups). It also furnishes a clue to the origins of the college and explains the extensive size of the parish. Norman takeover of the church in the country was largely accomplished by simply replacing Saxon clergy. Ousting an existing 'convent' and reconstituting the minster as a collegiate church covering the townships and chapelries of the parish (including Amington, Bonehill, Coton, Syerscote, Wigginton with Comberford and Wilnecote) would be consistent with Norman practice. By the time the first dean, William Marmion, is recorded in 1252, it is the lord of the castle who is in charge of making appointments. After the death of Philip Marmion, the Frevilles expected to inherit this privilege along with the castle, but Edward III successfully challenged their patronage, enabling St Editha's to become a royal free chapel, its clergy drawn from the sovereign's retinue and part of the royal household.

The Collegiate Church and the Reformation

Whatever may have existed before the Conquest was completely rebuilt in the years that followed. Norman churches followed a standard cruciform pattern, being built in the shape of a cross, the Christian symbol. Norman masons built for strength. Walls were firmly buttressed. Two immensely solid arches, simply decorated with zigzag moulding, remain of four that were built to carry the weight of a central crossing tower. Inside, the walls were plastered and brightly painted with a variety of vigorous scenes depicting biblical events and fanciful visions of damnation, designed to inspire a largely illiterate congregation. If typical, the east end would originally have been semicircular, not square as it is now, and at the west entrance would have been a narthex or porch stretching the width of the church. Here, rather than in the main body of the building, is where baptisms, churchings and wedding services were conducted and where penitents were reconciled.

A prebendal system is not mentioned before 1267 but if Tamworth followed the pattern at Lichfield and Wolverhampton this would have been introduced around 1140. As prebendaries, the dean and five canons each received tithes from one of the townships that came under the collective wing of the collegiate church. In addition to tithes from deanery lands, there was income from donations and from an annual St Editha's or Cherry Fair held in July. Tithes were frequently paid in kind and had to be stored for use or resale. A tithe barn or dean's barn stood on land beside Castle Orchard to the north-west of Aldergate. Gifts, endowments

42 *Norman arch, St Editha's church. Two massively solid, simply decorated Norman arches remain of four that were originally designed to carry the weight of a tower above the central crossing where nave, chancel and transepts intersect.*

43 & 44 *Interior of St Editha's church (1829), print from an engraving by Etienne Bruno Hamel (1796-1865) showing St Editha's after renovation, with replacement pews throughout and the nave flagged. Hamel noted at the time that 'although capable of containing three thousand persons, its revenue is lamentably small'; and Seal of St Editha's church. Replica of the pre-Reformation seal is above the entrance to the porch and repeated in the modern door handles. A Virgin and Child preside over an archbishop, two bishops and St Catherine holding the wheel and sword with which she was martyred. The initials TP stand for Thomas Parker, Dean of the College 1525-38.*

45 *The Deanery wall. Destroyed by fire in 1559, two crumbling stretches of ragstone wall interspersed with tile between the churchyard and Lower Gungate are all that remain above ground. Filled in cellars lie buried beneath the gardens.*

and annuities were given in return for prayers and requiem masses. Church income reflected the modest means of the local area but the dean lived relatively well. The deanery, between the churchyard and Lower Gungate, was a building of considerable size with vaulted cellars.

The great fire of 1345 left the church in ruins. In 1347, Baldwin de Witney took over as dean and over the next two decades supervised reconstruction. The central tower, possibly rendered unsafe by the fire, was not replaced. Early in the 15th century the familiar square tower was added to a remodelled west end. Plans for a spire to surmount the tower were shelved when doubts were raised about the ability of the foundations to support the extra weight. Inside the tower is an ingenious twin-spiral staircase, a double helix winding around a shared central newel post. With Pontefract and Much Wenlock, it is one of only three similar designs in the country. Separate doorways allow entry from inside or outside the church and the flights do not interconnect, an arrangement that allows someone to climb the tower while another descends, with neither person meeting the other. It was probably designed to enable use of the tower as a look-out point by the watch, without giving access into the church. Passages within the tower walls lead to window slits affording good views over the town.

Later in the 15th century the church was re-roofed, flattening the steep pitch and adding a clerestory to flood the nave with natural light. A small chantry chapel in the north transept was extended to become the North or St George's Chapel. The aisles were widened and the external crypt brought into the main body of the church.

It would be hard to overstate the importance of the medieval church. Religion was a literal truth, an everyday fact of life. St Editha's was a common focal point, perhaps especially so in a town administratively divided, and the only public building capable of holding a large assembly. Mystery plays probably took place in the nave and aisles and some of the court leet meetings were held in the church. Chancel, quire and the principal altar were reserved for the canons and screened from the main body of the church. Several altars were set up in the aisles and transepts for lay people. Wardens of the lights, elected annually, were responsible for keeping candles burning at these altars and for collecting alms and gifts to pay for a priest to officiate at services. Holding other jobs within the royal household meant that canons were absent for long periods. Pastoral responsibilities were delegated to vicars and deacons who were paid a pittance out of the prebendal income and subject to dismissal at short notice. One dean who took his job seriously was Dean John Bate. In 1442, he raised annual stipends and ensured the vicars had long-term job security. To help ease the pressure of work he persuaded Henry VI to provide for two additional chaplains, an agreement that seems to have conveniently slipped Henry's mind because the promised funds never arrived. Vicars lodged with local families until 1470, when one of the town bailiffs, Henry Jekes, gave them a place of their own. The communal house was in College Lane, then known as Cocket's Lane (after a local family of that name). Deacons were allowed to have their meals in the house but were required to sleep in the church, where they doubled as nightwatchmen.

Religious guilds, social organisations founded by tradespeople or merchants for charitable, educational and occasionally political purposes, were a feature of life in most medieval towns. A guild in Tamworth had its own Guildhall in Lower Gungate on the site later occupied by Guy's Almshouses. Shortly before the Reformation led to the dissolution of guilds along with chantries, the local guild members were in a position to pay for a priest whose duties combined celebrating mass in St George's Chapel and running the Free Grammar School for boys. It was not the first recorded gift left to support St George's Chantry, and a 'Schoolhouse Lane' between Gungate and the churchyard mentioned in the court rolls for 1384 implies that a school was already in existence at that date. Education had always come under the auspices of the Church so whether chapel and school were both founded by the guild or the school established as part of the college is not clear.

When Henry VIII declared himself Supreme Head of the Church of England in 1534, divorce from Catherine of Aragon and marriage to Anne Boleyn rather than Reformation of the Church was uppermost on his agenda. Nevertheless, some change was looking necessary. A wealthy and influential Church was increasingly envied by the middle classes. Papal authority was resented by the state. Pastoral care was patchy and a cause of dissatisfaction. Until the Reformation, services were conducted in Latin, a language not understood by the majority of the population. Bible-reading was not encouraged and printed English bibles were unavailable. When the Tyndale and Coverdale versions appeared in 1535, the new bibles were instantly popular, swiftly ran to several editions and prompted many to learn to read. Anglicisation of the liturgy began and in 1549 the Book of Common Prayer was published. Roman Catholic images were taken away and the rood screen was removed, along with the canons' stalls in the quire. Mystery plays were banned as superstitious nonsense and decorated walls were whitewashed over. A single communion table replaced the various altars.

Royal commissioners visited all parish churches to value their assets. During 1547-8 the college at Tamworth was dissolved and the school disendowed. The crown appropriated all St Editha's revenues and the prebendal lands belonging to the chapter were annexed. In compensation the last dean, Simon Symonds, and the prebends then in office received pensions. Under the life tenure agreed by Dean Bate over a century earlier the vicars could not be dismissed but in the event they too chose to step down and accept an annuity. St Editha's was allowed to remain as a parish church with a vicar and two curates to be appointed by the Crown.

The Post-Reformation Church

Parish registers were begun in 1558. Entries demonstrate how Catholics and noncon-formists, or dissenters, began to be excluded after the Reformation. Burial in consecrated ground was denied to those who did not accept the doctrines of the Church of England. An entry in the register for 1606 tells that William Tomlinson, a 'Papist', was buried in a ditch. In 1614, Ellen Aucott was amongst a privileged few refusing to attend Church of England services who was allowed to be laid to rest in St Editha's churchyard. Even so, the interment was only permitted to take place without ceremony and after dark.

In 1546, the Chantry Commissioners described Tamworth as one of four places in Staffordshire where there was most need of a hospital for relief of the poor, yet two years later the Spital Chapel closed and was sold as a private residence. The Vaughton family acquired some of the lands attached to the chapel. In 1855, Spital Chapel briefly became part of a mission college but then fell into disrepair. It was rescued and restored by the church authorities in 1914. A stone altar that had been dumped outside, possibly a sepulchre dating from the 'Sarum' rites practised in medieval times before the Tridentine mass was widely adopted, was brought back into pride of place.

In 1559, the deanery was destroyed by fire. Two stretches of crumbling ragstone wall are all that survive of the building above ground.

In Tudor England a newly emerged middle class of wealthy merchants and lawyers was eager to invest in real estate. When the crown began to dispose of vast tracts of Church property acquired as a result of the Reformation there was something of a speculative frenzy. The enormous wealth of the Church could have been channelled into poor relief or extended education provision; instead it lined the coffers of the Crown. Church holdings were auctioned off, sometimes to the highest bidder but often snapped up by well-connected crown servants. In the scramble, the deanery prebends with attached rights to appoint a vicar and curates at Tamworth were bought and sold on. Queen Elizabeth's 1588 Charter of Incorporation assured a future for the Free Grammar School as Queen Elizabeth's Grammar School, by confirming funding for a schoolmaster to be paid out of the crown revenues for Staffordshire. It also complicated the situation further by granting the new Corporation the right to appoint a vicar as well as a schoolmaster, two posts that were usually combined. In fact, the right to appoint a vicar to the living at St Editha's church had been privately sold seven years earlier and subsequently bought by Thomas Repington of Amington Hall. He refused to surrender patronage and an uneasy double election took place every time a new incumbent had to be found: Repington and his heirs proposed a candidate for the post of vicar; the Corporation then confirmed the applicant as schoolmaster. The two curate posts were offered to the same man, an arrangement that allowed the vicar the option of taking on extra duties and pocketing the stipends or appointing his own choice of assistants.

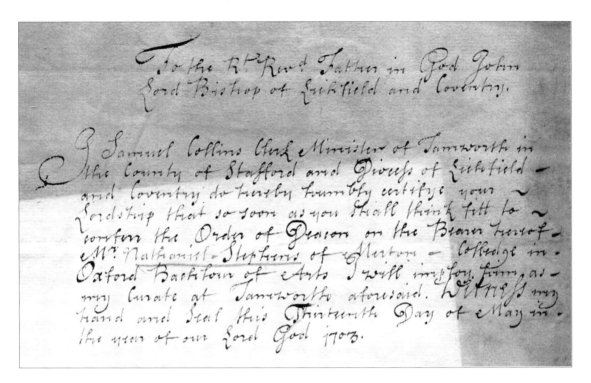

46　*Letter from the Reverend Samuel Collins, 1703.*
The posts of vicar and schoolmaster were usually combined,
the appointment requiring agreement between the
Corporation and the Repingtons of Amington Hall. The
vicar chose his own assistants and here writes to the
diocesan bishop requesting formal approval of his candidate
for the position of deacon.

When a vacancy occurred in 1758, the
Corporation decided to challenge this long-
standing but unwieldy system and moved
quickly to install the Reverend Simon Collins,
but Edward Repington had other ideas. He
refused to confirm the appointment of
Collins and put forward an alternative
candidate, the Reverend William Sawney.
Both sides refused to give way and the case
went before Stafford Assizes where
Repington won. Sawney took up his post as
vicar while Collins continued as schoolmaster
and the decision was tested at appeal. As
proceedings dragged on legal costs mounted.

47　*Church Street and St Editha's (1829), another of*
E.B. Hamel's series of illustrations. The railings erected
around the church in 1821 were removed in 1968 to enable
the pavement to be widened.

48 *Pew rights. Townspeople were expected to rent their seat in church. A few places in the outer aisles were set aside for those unable to pay. This 1793 certificate confirms a seat on pew number 61 in the north gallery for Nathaniel Wright.*

49 *The Reverend Brooke Lambert (1834-1901), radical vicar of Tamworth from 1872-8 and enthusiastic social reformer.*

In 1765, the Corporation was forced to mortgage property to cover lawyers' fees, lost its enthusiasm and decided to cut its losses. By the time the case reached the ultimate authority of the House of Lords in 1771, Collins found himself facing the appeal costs alone. He admitted defeat and withdrew his claim. William Sawney continued as vicar of St Editha's until 1792.

In 1809 St Editha's hosted an ambitious music festival to raise funds. A new organ had recently been installed and a rolling programme of renovation had seen the nave flagged, a new entrance made beneath the bell tower and replacement pews installed throughout. A few places in the outer aisles were set aside for those unable to pay but townspeople were expected to rent their seat in church. The event took place over Friday and Saturday, 21-22 September. One hundred and thirty musicians were involved, including some of the best-known names from the concert halls of London. Handel's *Messiah* opened proceedings, a performance of *The Creation* by Haydn followed, and a grand concert of sacred music with a double choir on stage brought celebrations to a climactic close.

In 1837, Charles Repington died, leaving Amington Hall and patronage of the deanery to his cousin, Captain Edward à Court, who was elected Member of Parliament for Tamworth in the same year.

Spiritual provision in Tamworth struggled to keep pace with change during the middle part of the 19th century. A growing population, industrialisation, the large size of the parish, falling revenues, the constant need for repairs, and the rise in nonconformity all posed problems for the parish church.

50 *The Reverend William MacGregor (1848-1936), vicar of Tamworth 1878-87. One of the town's great benefactors, he was a lifelong campaigner for social welfare, education and opportunities for self-improvement.*

51 *Tamworth Free Library catalogue. William MacGregor revived the public library after it had been forced to close due to lack of funds. This page from a catalogue shows the popularity of historical biography in Victorian Tamworth.*

Nonconformists objected to paying church rates towards the upkeep of churches they didn't use, and churchwardens at St Editha's took legal action when a local dissenter refused to pay. Tamworth gained a national reputation for the strength of its opposition to compulsory church rates. In 1867 the town levy was ruled illegal by the Court of Arches, forcing the church to fall back on fund raising and voluntary contributions for its upkeep.

The Reverend Richard Rawle, appointed in 1869, resigned after only three years in post, remarking pointedly there were no attractions to Tamworth but the work. Into the breach stepped Brooke Lambert, with William MacGregor in support as curate for Hopwas, specifically to tackle the difficulties facing the

52   *Tamworth Co-operative Society, Colehill. William MacGregor's support enabled a society to become established in 1886 in the face of opposition from local traders.*

53   *The Reverend Brooke Lambert memorial window, St Editha's church. By William Morris, leader of the Arts and Crafts movement, to a design by Edward Burne-Jones, this memorial window is in St George's chapel.*

parish. Both were single men of independent means and wealthy enough to make the stipend irrelevant, an important point given the poverty of the livings. Lambert and MacGregor were enthusiastic liberals committed to public investment in pursuit of social welfare, education and opportunities for self-improvement. They shared a pragmatic approach to nonconformism, forging ecumenical links with other denominations in pursuit of mutual aims. This lack of respect for convention was a cause for concern amongst some of St Editha's more reactionary Anglican parishioners.

Lambert masterminded a takeover of the recently launched *Tamworth Herald* and introduced a parish magazine. A policy of objective neutrality was maintained at the *Herald,* but the parish magazine was used persuasively. Details of church collections were published in an attempt to shame those in the congregation who could afford to do so into digging a little deeper. Plans for a cottage hospital were instigated.

MacGregor moved from his parish post at Hopwas to take up a living in Liverpool. When Brooke Lambert was forced to resign in 1878, after the family fortunes nosedived, MacGregor returned to succeed him and continue the work of social reform begun in the town, including financing the completion of the hospital.

MacGregor paid for the building of St George's Institute and indoor baths in Church Street, where young people could attend lessons in art and science, keep fit in the gymnasium and swim. He helped revive a free library and campaigned vigorously for increased public investment in health and education services.

54   *Church bells removed for recasting. In addition to announcing that services were about to begin, church bells were once rung to signal time for bed and time to rise. In 1932, the six bells were removed for recasting and additions made. In this picture are Mr G. Perry (churchwarden), Miss W. Chaplin (bellringer) and Mr H. Chaplin (verger).*

In 1886, MacGregor lent his support to moves to form a co-operative society, offering his services as treasurer and providing premises on a lease. Societies had been tried earlier in Fazeley (1865) and Wilnecote (1872) but both attempts proved short-lived. With MacGregor's support the Tamworth society established itself and began trading. A cartel of existing small shopkeepers fiercely opposed to this competition responded by organising a boycott of the church. Caught in the backlash, MacGregor resigned. He had been ill and the poor state of his health was given as the official reason for leaving.

For his retirement, MacGregor built Bolehall Manor in Glascote Road. Beside each doorway in the house he inscribed an apt prayer. Above the main entrance is carved 'Worlds above and worlds below, mansions are they all of the Great Father's house'. He continued to be active in town affairs, taking over Lambert's interest in the *Herald*, serving as chairman of the Savings Bank and Tamworth Building Society, and as a school governor. For almost three decades he was also a Warwickshire county councillor.

Under the stewardship of Lambert and MacGregor, St Editha's church was lovingly restored and enhanced. Local craftsmen, individuals who took a pride in their work, were employed on repairs instead of contractors from outside the area. Exquisite stained glass, commissioned from leading members of the new Arts and Crafts movement, augmented the beauty of the building.

The last lay dean was Mr C.H. Repington. Shortly before his death, in 1903, responsibility for presenting the vicar transferred to the diocesan bishop at Lichfield. Prebendal accountability for upkeep and maintenance of the church was taken over by the churchwardens.

Nonconformism

Protestants who did not conform to the doctrines of the new Church of England were treated as recusants, and subject to persecution in the same way as Catholics. Many Puritans believed the changes introduced did not go far enough. Now that English bibles were available, there were those who considered reading the scriptures gave them a direct line to the Almighty, removing the need for priests with their ceremonies and sacraments. With the end of the Commonwealth and the monarchy restored, Puritanism became less extreme and adherents merged with other nonconformist sects. Many Presbyterians and Baptists became Unitarians, a group with progressive views who accepted Christ as God's human messenger but not as divine. The Toleration Act of 1689 allowed more freedom of worship and the Whig Party, an emerging political influence, championed religious as well as civil liberty.

A group of Unitarians held their inaugural meeting in Tamworth in 1690. The congregation grew and in 1724 built the first nonconformist church in town in what was then a field behind Colehill.

George Fox, a Warwickshire man born in Fenny Drayton in 1647, founded the Quaker movement. His Society of Friends

55 *Unitarian chapel, Victoria Road. The first nonconformist chapel in Tamworth was built in 1724 in an open field. The building is now shared with the local Royal Naval Association branch.*

renounced formal services, paid clergy and what they saw as the superstitious ritual of the established church. For a century from the early 1750s, a meeting house stood behind 101 Lichfield Street. Twenty Quakers received simple burials in the garden there.

Evangelical Methodism arrived in 1771. Local man Samuel Watton invited preachers to address groups of people in his home. Until 1795, Methodism was still officially part of the Church of England. The first Methodist church opened in Bolebridge Street in 1816, to be followed by other chapels as differences of opinion led to splinter groups of Primitives, Wesleyans and other sub-denominations. In 1869, local philanthropist Elizabeth Hutton of Dosthill Hall, herself a regular member of the congregation at St Editha's, endowed a mission hall in Bolebridge Street as an informal place of worship for those uncomfortable with denominational dogma.

Five

MUNICIPAL UNITY: INCORPORATION, PLAGUE AND CIVIL WAR

Smooth running of the borough depended upon a close working relationship between the Staffordshire and Warwickshire sides of the town. Both had their own Town Hall: Staffordshire on the south side of Lichfield Street; Warwickshire on the north side of Market Street. The Warwickshire hall was most probably on the site later occupied by the *King's Arms*, which became the *Peel Arms* and is now Wilkinson's retail store. Courts met separately under bailiffs elected for each side of the borough but their activities were co-ordinated and all revenues went into the 'towne box', as the common chest was popularly known. Administratively, each side of the town was a mirror image of the other. If the division of the town did not cause any particular problems there were still obvious benefits to be gained from coming together as a single unit, removing duplication and rationalising the running of the borough. As other towns prospered and grew, Tamworth's relative decline as a centre of importance raised a question mark over its standing. Markets and fairs continued but other privileges associated with borough status, such as the right to representation in Parliament, had never been exercised. It was a position that needed to be rectified and a petition was submitted to the Crown.

On Christmas Eve 1560, Elizabeth I approved plans to unify the town under a central executive body. A Charter of Incorporation was granted, formally acknowledging Tamworth as a legal borough by prescription based on ancient precedent and rights established in the distant, unrecorded past. The town's existing privileges were confirmed in their entirety by the document, including the right to hold markets, courts and the two fairs granted by Edward III in 1337. An additional court, the Court Baron, was set up to deal with issues of service arising between the lord of the manor and his tenants and to handle small personal claims.

The appointment of two sergeants of the mace was authorised, adding a touch of ceremonial pomp to formal occasions. Accompanying the bailiff as he carried out his civic duties, the mace-bearer made official announcements and had nominal powers of arrest.

A Corporation of 'the bailiffs and commonalty' was constituted. This single governing body was to have two bailiffs, a reduction from the four required under the previous system, and 24 capital burgesses 'of the best and most honest inhabitants of the borough'. The post of official taster was

a single Court of Record formed to replace the two portmanmoot courts. The chamberlains managed the court receipts which were the Corporation's prime source of revenue.

Warwickshire's Town Hall on Market Street became the common meeting place for the new Corporation until it was replaced in 1701. When repairs to this later building were carried out in 1896, a strip of oak panelling was discovered, probably belonging to the old meeting hall. On it were carved the names of chamberlains Robert Peake and Cornelius Osborne beneath a single fleur-de-lys, and the date 1672. A fleur-de-lys became part of the town's official crest from 1679, when new Member of Parliament Sir Thomas Thynne celebrated his election by presenting the borough with its own seal. Earlier associations of the symbol with Tamworth may date back to 1337 and the grant of two fairs by Edward III. Edward added this traditional heraldic device of the French kings to his own arms in pursuit of his claim to the throne of France.

The new Corporation did not win universal approval. As a largely unaccountable and self-perpetuating body, its new powers led to problems. A raft of corruption allegations reached the ears of both the Earl of Essex and Humphrey Ferrers. Bailiffs were accused of abusing their position by accepting bribes in return for dropping charges and misappropriating stolen goods.

abolished. Capital burgesses were installed for life and were jointly responsible for choosing replacements when a vacancy occurred. Bailiffs were elected annually on 1 August to serve for one year. They in turn appointed two chamberlains to serve the same term in office. One of the bailiffs' main responsibilities was to act as Justices of the Peace, officiating at a merged Court Leet and

Disputes arose over the rights claimed by the borough. William Comberford believed his position as lord of the manor of Wigginton, inherited from his Hastings relatives, included the Staffordshire part of the town and it took a protracted legal battle before the Corporation was able to assert ownership. When Sir Walter Aston, lord of the manor of Bolehall, allowed his tenants to put large numbers of sheep on Warwickshire

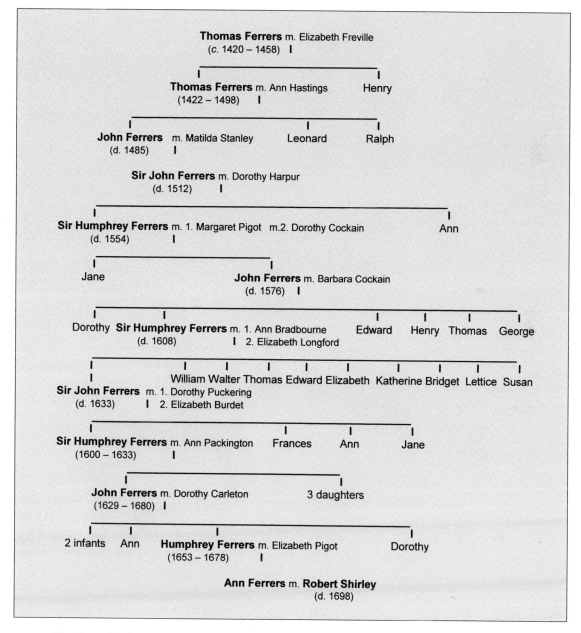

57 *The Ferrers family. Sir Thomas Ferrers, 5th Earl Ferrers of Groby, inherited Tamworth Castle through marriage to Elizabeth Freville. The castle remained in Ferrers hands until 1688 when it passed to the Shirley family of Chartley Manor.*

58   *The* Moat House, *Lichfield Street. Originally known as Moat Hall, it was rebuilt in the latest Elizabethan style with stepped gables and a battlemented tower around 1572. Now it is a restaurant.*

Moor the Corporation faced another fight to protect householders' rights of pasture on the common.

Humphrey Ferrers had his own arguments with the townspeople, many of whom were boycotting Castle Mill and grinding grain at home using hand querns. Ferrers claimed the loss of business threatened the viability of his operation and gained a court injunction forcing local people to take their corn to his mill.

Three years after incorporation the borough returned direct representatives to parliament for the first time. The election of brothers Michael and Robert Harcourt was probably prompted as much by the jockeying for power between various local factions than by any sudden reawakening of civic duty. Technically responsibility for election rested with the 24 capital burgesses; in practice the lords at the castle and at Drayton Bassett, together with the county sheriff,

directed the choice of candidates and exercised what was in effect a political monopoly.

At the time of the election in 1563, another member of the Harcourt family, Walter, was living at Moat Hall in Lichfield Street, one of a number of properties owned by the Comberford family. Walter had moved in when he married Humphrey Comberford's daughter, Mary. Richard, Joan and John Jekes had contested ownership of the property in 1554 but settled for a lump sum. Mary and Walter were probably living there when the house was rebuilt in the latest grand Elizabethan style, incorporating a battlemented tower, around 1572. When the Jekes family renewed their claim, offering to return with interest the money they had accepted earlier, the case went to court, where Comberford won a conclusive decision. The redesigned Moat Hall soon became known as the Moat House.

Various Acts of Uniformity following the Reformation prescribed penalties for those not attending the new Church of England services. Initially the penalty was one shilling per offence, but in 1581, after the Pope had declared attendance a mortal sin, it rose to a punitive £20 a month. Both the Comberfords and the Harcourts were recusants. Their public refusal to renounce the Roman Catholic faith put the Comberford Chapel in the north transept of St Editha's, built at Comberford expense following the great fire of 1345, out of bounds. Members of the two families were regularly fined for non-attendance at church.

'Priest holes', secret chambers where priests smuggled into the house to say mass could be concealed if necessary, may have been a design feature of the new Moat Hall. After the death of Mary Harcourt in 1591, William Comberford made the mansion his main home. In 1606, acting on a tip-off, Sir Humphrey Ferrers sent the bailiffs with a number of his servants to search the Moat House. Protestations and locked doors were ignored as guests were interrogated and the men went through each room banging on panelling. Three strangers were discovered hiding and arrested on suspicion of being seminaries. Clerical vestments found beneath a bed were also seized along with religious texts. Despite the weight of circumstantial evidence there was no hard proof that mass was being celebrated.

A high steward, appointed to preside over the Corporation, represented the interests of the Crown. As lords of Tamworth Castle, the Ferrers traditionally filled the role almost by default. It was an honorary position and not one that seems to have carried much status or been taken very seriously. A year after the death of John Ferrers in 1576, his son Humphrey was appointed to the office. But there was a new kid on the block. Sir Robert Devereux, 2nd Earl of Essex, was inheritor of Chartley Hall, formerly part of the Ferrers estates that had been subject to division in the 15th century. Robert's widowed mother Lettice Knolleys had married Sir Robert Dudley, Earl of Leicester. Her son was a regular visitor at their Drayton Bassett home. The dashing young Earl took an interest in local affairs and used his influence as Queen Elizabeth's favourite courtier to obtain a second charter for the town in 1588, consolidating the earlier grant and adding important further concessions. Under its terms the Corporation became 'guardians and governors' of the grammar school, the Cherry Fair, not held since the winding up of the college, was revived, and revenues lost to the Treasury when the chantry chapel of St George was dissolved were restored. When the charter was granted the Earl of Essex was named as high steward by Elizabeth's chief minister, William Cecil, Lord Burghley. An aggrieved Humphrey Ferrers contested the decision, eventually taking his case before the Privy Council, whose members refused to reverse the appointment. Being high steward gave Devereux the opportunity to promote those close to him. In the year the new charter was issued the Corporation returned Sir Robert's younger brother, Edward Devereux, and the family tutor, Robert Wright, as Members of Parliament for the town.

On 30 April 1599, the Earl of Essex left to lead an army against the Irish rebel Hugh O'Neill. St Editha's parish register records

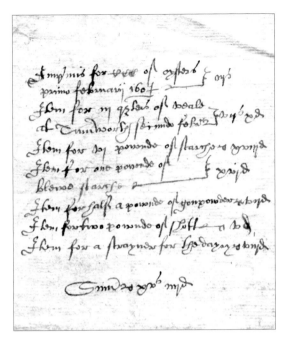

59 *Itemised bill from the household accounts of Sir Humphrey Ferrers. In February 1604: 3,000 oysters (3s.); three quarters of veal (7s. 10d.); six pounds of starch (18d.); one pound of blue starch (16d.); half a pound of gunpowder (7d.); two pounds of shot (5d.); and a strainer for the dairy (8d.); cost 15s. 4d.*

that Robert 'went fro' Drayton Bassett toward Ireland wh an hoste of men to make Warre against ye Earle of Tyrone'. It turned into a low-key campaign lasting five months and concluded by an unsatisfactory truce, after which Devereux returned to England against the Queen's wishes. Dissatisfied with the Earl's performance against the Irish rebels, Elizabeth ordered him to be detained and Devereux found himself temporarily imprisoned. On his release he tried to raise a force against the Queen, was arrested and, in 1601, executed for high treason. Edward Devereux, William Comberford and Robert Wright were also suspected of being implicated in the plot against Elizabeth but no evidence against them emerged.

Ferrers, by now Sir Humphrey, expected the newly vacant high stewardship of Tamworth to be his but instead Sir John Egerton was given the post. Egerton's appointment was due purely to political patronage. He had no connection with the town and the Corporation backed Sir Humphrey's claim. Another lengthy process of appeal began. Just when it seemed as though matters would be resolved in favour of Ferrers he died, leaving his son John to benefit.

Plague and Poverty

Despite the problems that punctuated the early years, incorporation marked a new beginning and enabled Tamworth to take advantage of the opportunities for trade and development available to an ambitious town in Elizabethan England. The borough had grown to around 300 households but not everyone prospered. Between rich and poor there was a widening gap. Disease and destitution posed a constant threat.

Repeated outbreaks of plague struck at regular intervals in the years between 1556 and 1626, robbing children of parents and families of breadwinners. The bacteria responsible are a parasite of rats and mice. Rodent fleas transmitted the bubonic form of the disease to humans, whose coughs and sneezes spread a pneumonic infection. Once the disease caught hold poor sanitary conditions and cramped housing led to epidemics. An entry in the parish register for 1597-8 tersely records 'Dyvers died of ye blouddie flixe'.

A number of residents bequeathed money or property in their wills to provide help for the poor, nominating either the Corporation or the Church authorities to be responsible for administration. But individual philanthropy and voluntary subscriptions were failing to meet needs. Government passed a series of Poor Laws amid concerns about a potential threat to public order. For the first time a distinction was made between the 'deserving' and the so-called 'undeserving' poor. Local taxes to pay for poor relief became compulsory in 1572. Setting and collecting a poor rate was the responsibility of the Church, giving the ecclesiastical parish a civic function. The Relief of the Poor Act (1601) required every parish to have overseers of the poor whose job it was to administer relief. The overseers were appointed by Justices of the Peace and usually included the churchwardens. Landowners and businesses were required to contribute. It was a system that made each local community responsible for its own people, but after the plague epidemic of 1626 conditions were so wretched in Tamworth that Warwickshire County Assizes ordered a county-wide levy to help alleviate the suffering caused by poverty in the town.

Civil War

James I, son of Mary, Queen of Scots, became the first Stuart king of England in 1603. He visited Tamworth on three occasions. On his initial visit in 1619, Prince Charles accompanied him. James stayed with Sir John Ferrers, who claimed shared descent from

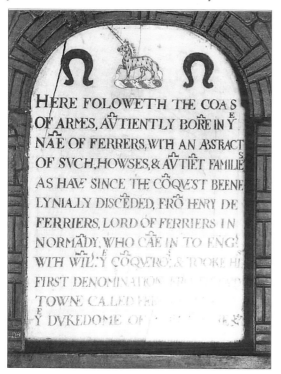

60 *Ferrers frieze, Tamworth Castle. The first of 55 early 19th-century heraldic panels showing the coats of arms of the Ferrers family through the ages that form a frieze around the state withdrawing room of the castle.*

61 *Ferrers heraldic panel, Tamworth Castle. One of three panels above the 17th-century fireplace in the state withdrawing room of the castle, showing the shared descent of James I and Sir John Ferrers.*

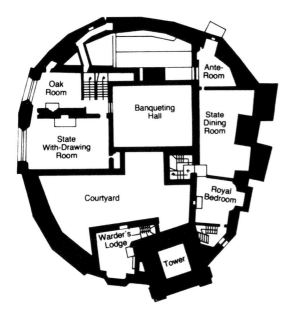

62 *Castle floor plan. A 13th-century hall in the first-floor north wing was divided by close-studded timber partitions to make the royal bedchamber and state dining room, with a small ante-room leading off, in preparation for the visit of James I in 1619.*

63 *Royal bedchamber, Tamworth Castle. James I visited the castle in 1619, 1621 and 1624. He is reported to have slept in this first-floor room. The four-poster bed is a more recent addition, on loan from the Victoria and Albert Museum.*

David I of Scotland. Charles was the guest of William Comberford at the Moat House. The parish register noted, 'The kinge lodged at ye castell; and ye prince at the motall. Mr Thomas Ashley and Mr John Sharp, then beilieffes, gave royall entertaynement.' In preparation for the visit, Sir John renovated the early 13th-century hall on the first floor of the north wing of the castle. Two large bay windows with balconies were added and the open room was partitioned to create a state drawing-room with a small ante-room at one end and a royal bedchamber leading off at the other.

Charles became king in 1625. Constitutional and religious differences between the monarch and Parliament soon became apparent and in 1642 resulted in civil war. William Comberford raised a small royalist force and garrisoned the castle for his sovereign, from where he was well placed to raid opposing forces. John Ferrers, a royal ward since the death of his father nine years earlier, was a boy of just 13 years. He and his family retreated ten miles north to the family house at Walton-on-Trent for the duration. Nearby Lichfield was held by Parliament. Many of the gentry raised militia and pressed their tenants into service. Recruiting officers marched through the countryside with military bandsmen at their side literally drumming up business. Soldiers' pay was attractive compared with the wages on offer for a general labourer.

Both sides raised money by local levies and quartered men in private homes. Those who paid their taxes were promised exemption from other contributions but horses were still commandeered, depriving farmers of the means to work their land.

A short two-day siege in June 1643 resulted in the capture of the castle by a detachment of Cromwell's forces under Colonel William Purefoy. Comberford escaped but many of the garrison remained as prisoners. The castle suffered little damage in the attack and a small force was left in control under the governorship of Captain Waldyve Willington. Comberford's home, the Moat House, was plundered and the Comberford Chapel defaced.

As the fortunes of the opposing sides seesawed, Lichfield fell to the royalists, who tried but failed to recapture Tamworth. Concerned about the need to strengthen his defences, Captain Willington prevailed upon the Earl of Denbigh to requisition a saker (a large artillery piece) and two smaller field cannons known as drakes for the castle. Insults were exchanged between the two sides. One of Willington's officers, Thomas Hunt, called Colonel Henry Bagot, commander of the royalist forces at Lichfield, the 'son of a whore' and challenged him to a duel. Despite constant skirmishes between the opposing factions parliamentarian forces remained in control at Tamworth. Meanwhile the balance of power was slowly shifting.

Supplemented by Scots forces, Oliver Cromwell's New Model Army gained a decisive victory at Naseby in June 1645. Three weeks later an army of Scots camped at Tamworth, helping themselves to geese, poultry and other supplies. Soldiers lodging with Tamworth resident John Robins not only failed to pay what they owed for their keep but also accidentally set his house alight.

In spring 1646 a large parliamentarian force backed by soldiers from the Tamworth garrison surrounded the royalists blockaded

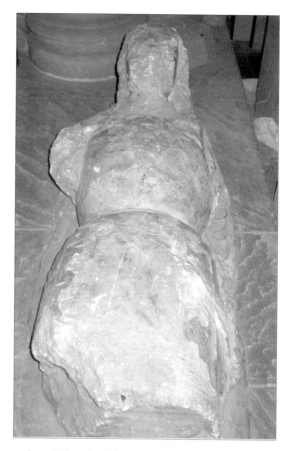

64 *Effigy, St Editha's church. The parish church suffered at the hands of Parliamentary forces occupying Tamworth during the Civil War. This mutilated freestone monument in the north transept of St Editha's is thought to be a member of the Comberford family.*

65 *Cannon, Castle Grounds. Captain Waldyve Willington, in charge of the garrison at Tamworth Castle in the Civil War, ordered extra artillery, including two drakes, to strengthen his defences. A drake was a light field piece with a tapering bore.*

66 *Comberford memorial, St Editha's church. This tablet in the north transept of St Editha's – the Comberford Chapel – records the death of the last of the English line, Robert Comberford, in 1671 and mourns 'the once flourishing family who did so much for the town'.*

in the Cathedral Close, Lichfield. After a fierce siege lasting four months, during which the royalist commander Colonel Bagot was badly wounded, they eventually succeeded in recapturing the city.

When the war was finally over, the survival of Tamworth Castle was again at risk, just as it had been in 1215 when threatened by an angry King John. The Council of State issued orders for it to be destroyed. Once more the command was never carried out. Members of the Comberford family fled to Ireland. William Comberford's heir, his nephew Robert, was forced to sell the Moat House in 1654; ironically, the buyer was a former captain in the parliamentarian army, Thomas Fox.

From 1563 to 1640 the town had regularly returned parliamentary representatives to Westminster. At the last election before the outbreak of war, Fernando Stanhope, son of the Earl of Chesterfield and married to Catherine Hastings, had been one of those elected. He became a colonel of horse in the royalist army and was killed in 1644. When the conflict ended, Oliver Cromwell at first governed the new Republic through a Council of State and a purged 'Rump' of just 60 independent-minded radical MPs in the House of Commons. In 1653, this number was increased to 140 members, all hand picked by Cromwell. Tamworth, along with many other small boroughs, did not have a nominated representative. Ostensibly Cromwell's aim was to broaden representation, extending the right to be heard in Parliament to larger towns previously denied the privilege. Undoubtedly there was also an element of punishment for those towns that had shown sympathy for the royalist cause. John Swinfen, a career politician who had been MP for Stafford, was returned for Tamworth briefly in 1658, after Richard Cromwell had succeeded his father as Lord Protector. Within a year the 'Rump' was recalled and he was excluded. Normal business was not resumed until the Commonwealth had ended. With the monarchy restored, Tamworth's right to elect two parliamentary members was reinstated. In 1660, John Swinfen was elected together with John, Lord Clifford to represent the town.

Six

PATRONAGE AND CHARITY:
BEQUESTS AND BENEFACTORS

Charles II renewed the Town Charter in 1663, nominating James Compton, Earl of Northampton as high steward. The terms were unchanged except for an additional requirement that all members of the Corporation swear an oath of allegiance and the removal of legal red tape to allow further development of the grammar school.

Nationally it was a time of suspicion and intrigue. Rumours of plots and counter-plots circulated. Political parties began to emerge. The reforming 'Whig' Party, mainly landed gentry independent enough not to have to defer to the monarch in all matters, grew out of the Country Party. Local government was subject to scrutiny. When James II succeeded his brother he actively challenged the rights and privileges enjoyed by town corporations, demanding that smaller boroughs relinquish their charters. On the surface the intention was to take the administrative reins out of the hands of a few life appointees and establish a more democratic sharing of power at local level; in reality the purpose was to reduce opportunities for political opponents of the monarch to build a powerbase. Tamworth Corporation faced a dilemma: dispute the legality of James's action in the courts and face the consequences of challenging royal authority, or dutifully accede

and plead to be allowed to continue. They chose the course of least resistance, humbly beseeching his majesty 'to accept this our surrender, and doe with all submission to his majesties good pleasure, implore his grace and favour to regrant to us, the said bailiffs and commonalty, the naming and choosing of the said officers, and the said liberties and

67 *Royal seal of Charles II. King Charles renewed the Town Charter in 1663. From the time of Edward the Confessor each monarch had his own Great Seal that was affixed to Proclamations, Letters Patent and other official documents.*

privileges'. As a result a new charter was issued in 1688, replacing the corporate body with a mayor and 12 aldermen. Morgan Powell, the town clerk, was elected as the inaugural mayor. It proved a temporary change. Under increasing pressure to abdicate in favour of his daughter Mary and her husband William of Orange, James undid all the changes he had introduced in a belated attempt to win back support in the country at large.

A two-day ceremonial perambulation of the borough boundaries took place in 1697. Beating the bounds was a periodic and literal ritual to assert jurisdiction. Members of the Corporation led a procession around the town limits with frequent stops for refreshment. A group of young men were taken along and subjected to a whipping or a ducking as an aid to memory at key points along the way. The individuals concerned earning a penny or two as recompense for the experience.

Political patronage in the town was shared between the lords of the castle and of Drayton Bassett. Returning two representatives to Parliament allowed each to sponsor or nominate a candidate. Agreement avoided the expense of wining, dining and otherwise bribing the electorate, but it was not always straightforward. In 1670 John Ferrers stood against Charles, Lord Clifford. When he lost the election he appealed to the House of Commons on the grounds that all the burgesses of the town should be entitled to vote, not just the Corporation. A Commons Select Committee rejected his appeal but only narrowly. Change was on the way. By the end of the century the vote had been extended to all those who paid the local church and poor rates, known colloquially as 'scot and lot'. The franchise included non-residents who owned property of a certain value in the town. This added to the costs when elections were contested, political opponents competing to pay expenses for non-residents to be in town on polling day. From 1723 this qualification was revised to make residence mandatory, a move which gave a total electorate in Tamworth of around two hundred and fifty individuals.

When the 3rd Earl of Essex died childless his estates were divided between the heirs of his Devereux sisters, Frances and Dorothy. Lady Dorothy's share went to Robert Shirley who married Anne Ferrers and became Earl Ferrers and Viscount Tamworth. Neither Robert Shirley, nor his daughter Elizabeth, who inherited the castle along with her husband James Compton, 5th Earl of Northampton, chose to make their main home at Tamworth. Maintenance was neglected and the fabric of the castle began to deteriorate.

Sir Thomas Thynne, Viscount Weymouth from 1682, inherited Drayton Bassett from Lady Frances Devereux but moved to Wiltshire when Longleat came into his possession. Politically a supporter of the newly emerged political grouping known as 'Tories', Thynne served as Member of Parliament for the town from 1679-80 before taking over from Compton as high steward in 1681. At first Thynne opposed James II and was instrumental in early overtures addressed to William of Orange. He then changed his mind and backed the King, but he took his oath of allegiance when William and Mary were crowned in 1689.

In 1745 there was one last attempt to restore the Stuarts to the throne. Bonnie Prince Charlie raised an army and marched into England, formally declaring his father James III, King of England in the market place at Ashbourne, Derbyshire. The route chosen for the march on London deliberately cut through Staffordshire to give Charles an opportunity to pick up support. The county had a reputation for Jacobite sympathies. The Reverend William Paul, a former assistant master at the grammar school, had been hanged at Tyburn after the 1715 rising for publicly praying that James Edward Stuart succeeded. An advance guard was despatched to Tamworth and spent the night here, while delegates tried unsuccessfully to persuade the local gentry to sign up to their cause.

68 *George Townshend, 1st Marquis, Viscount Townshend of Raynham (1724-1807). Townshend had a distinguished military and political career and was an accomplished cartoonist.*

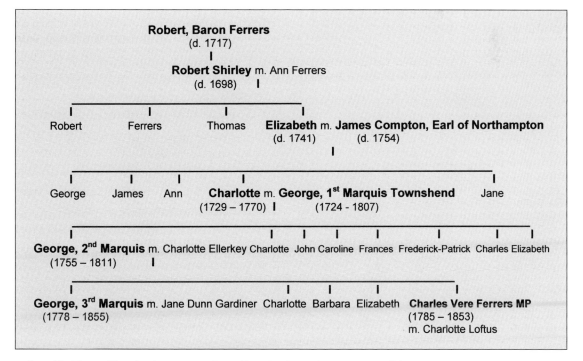

69 *The Ferrers-Townshend connection. George Townshend, 1st Marquis, inherited Tamworth Castle by marriage to Lady Charlotte Compton, daughter of Elizabeth Ferrers.*

George Townshend, 1st Marquis and Viscount Townshend of Raynham, was with the Duke of Cumberland when the Jacobite rebellion was crushed at the Battle of Culloden in 1746. Five years later he married Lady Charlotte Compton, the heir of Elizabeth Ferrers and James Compton, and in 1754 he inherited Tamworth Castle. Townshend had a distinguished military and political career, serving with General Wolfe in Quebec and becoming a Privy Councillor and Lord Lieutenant of Ireland. As a skilful caricaturist with a fair claim to being the first political cartoonist, his sketches were sufficiently caustic to offend some of those in public life who became the target of his wit.

By the second half of the 18th century, the control economy of the Middle Ages, when the weight and price of bread sold in the town was fixed by local statute, was a thing of the past. Prices now fluctuated according to the laws of supply and demand. Narrow tape manufacture had begun and the beginnings of a more industrial town were visible, but tanning remained a major source of business. Tamworth was still essentially a rural community. When the harvest failed after the wet summer of 1766, there was a shortage of corn. Prices of all foodstuffs rose. Some local supplies chased the higher prices available in London, thereby adding to problems. Towards the end of September, a crowd caught the national mood and took to the streets, attacking market traders in an attempt to force down the price of butter and other products. To restore order and prevent further riots, George Townshend and Thomas Thynne subsidised supplies, buying grain at the inflated market price, taking a loss and selling it to the inhabitants of the town at a price they could afford.

Bequests and Benefactors

In common with most towns of the day, Tamworth was heavily dependent on individual benefactors. When a new schoolroom and schoolhouse was built for the grammar school on Lower Gungate in 1678-9, the work was funded by voluntary contributions from former pupils and leading townspeople, including Thomas Guy, the Vaughtons, John Rawlett, Humphrey Ferrers and Thomas Thynne. A stone carving of a fleur-de-lys was placed above the entrance.

The Reverend John Rawlett was one of many natives of the town who donated gifts of money or property in their wills to be used for the benefit of the town. When he died in 1686, aged 44, he left money to found a school for poor children and a collection of almost a thousand books that found a home in a room of Guy's newly built almshouses and formed the basis of the first local library.

From 1662, everyone was required to have a parish of legal settlement. Individuals could qualify by residence, owning property, holding office, or after a continuous period of 365 days employment in the town. Each parish was legally responsible for the relief of poverty amongst its own residents. A Board of Guardians was elected, to whom the two overseers of the poor were now required to report. Money for relief was raised from a Poor Rate, collected from landowners and businesses, and from redirected court fines. Overseers were permitted to expel 'vagrants', a loose term that extended to anyone not officially a resident of Tamworth and considered to be

70 *Grammar school, Lower Gungate. A new schoolroom and schoolhouse were built when George Antrobus was master in 1678-9, paid for by voluntary contributions. The building was demolished in 1867.*

without the means of self-support. With perhaps one in five of the population living a hand-to-mouth existence, there were many who occasionally found themselves in need of help. Shame being seen as a deterrent in a small community, those unfortunates forced to go 'on the parish' were made to wear the brass letters TP, signifying 'Tamworth Pauper', prominently on their sleeve.

Illegitimacy was no big deal socially, but efforts were made to trace the fathers of children born to unmarried mothers, and filiation orders, known as 'bastardy bonds', were served requiring maintenance to be paid. Orphans and the children of poor families were a persistent burden on the funds raised for poor relief. Apprenticeships arranged

71 *Fleur-de-lys, Lower Gungate. Stone carving of the town symbol formerly above the entrance to the grammar school and now incorporated in the brickwork of shops built on the site in 1970.*

72   *Number 1, Lady Bank. Built as the Workhouse, it became Castle Brewery and then housed the Ministry of Labour before becoming an annexe of the Castle Hotel. The tall chimneys still have interior handles from the days when chimney boys climbed inside the stacks with scrapers and brushes to clear accumulated soot.*

elsewhere, even at parish expense, offered a solution since they transferred residency and, therefore, future responsibility providing the full period of indenture was served. Girls were apprenticed up to the age of 21 years unless terminated by marriage, in which case wives adopted their husband's parish. Boys did not usually qualify until they reached 24 years of age, making them attractive as cheap labour.

In 1687, a trust was set up to operate an institution for the poor children of the parish on land in Schoolhouse Lane donated by Thomas Thynne. Public contributions in cash and kind resulted in the Spinning School, where children from the age of five years were set to work spinning and knitting in return for board and keep. By 1719, the number of children entering had fallen and

the building was converted into accommodation for the poor.

Under the Workhouse Test Act of 1722, all individuals had to enter a workhouse in order to qualify for assistance. James Compton built premises on Gungate and gave them to the town in 1741. Just in case anyone was tempted to consider it a soft option, life in the workhouse was subject to a harsh regime. No distinction was made between able-bodied, disabled, sick or elderly. Inmates were expected to work to cover the costs of running the institution. Within a decade the Gungate building was too small to cope. Thomas Thynne and Francis Willoughby of Middleton Hall shared the cost of providing a replacement beside the Tame at Lady Bank.

In 1833, Earl Grey set up a national Poor Law Commission that led to major reform of the workhouse system. Instead of being individually responsible for poor relief, parishes were grouped into unions with a common workhouse under the supervision of a board of governors. Tamworth was at the centre of a union of 24 parishes. Despite a second building at Lady Bank, facilities soon proved inadequate. A new Union Workhouse was built off Wigginton Road and later became part of St Editha's Hospital. Conditions were still strict but now it was only the able-bodied poor who had to enter the workhouse in order to receive help. Others, such as the elderly and sick considered to be victims of circumstances beyond their control, were permitted relief in their own homes. Children were allowed to attend school outside the workhouse. The Poor Laws continued to dictate social policy until they were abolished by the National Assistance Act of 1948.

Thomas Guy

Thomas Guy was born in Southwark, London, the eldest of three children. He was around eight years of age when his father died in 1652 and his mother, Anne Vaughton, returned to her family home at Tamworth along with Thomas and his younger brother and sister. Generations of Vaughtons, who once occupied the Manor House in Lichfield Street, played a prominent role in the town. Members of the family served as bailiffs, chamberlains, churchwardens and in a variety of official and civic posts. There was a tradition of charitable giving in the family. Thomas was an able boy who made the most of an education at the grammar school,

73 *Thomas Guy (c.1644-1724). Lampooned as a miserly penny-pincher, much of Guy's charitable work only became known after his death.*

returning to London at the age of 15 or 16 to begin an apprenticeship with John Clark, a bookbinder and bookseller. Completion of an eight-year training period qualified him to become a freeman of the city and a liveryman of the Stationers' Company, and he opened a shop on the corner of Cornhill and Lombard Street. Guy showed considerable business acumen in what was still a relatively new and competitive trade. Publishing good quality bibles, prayer books and academic texts under his own imprint made him wealthy.

Although briefly engaged to one of his maids, Thomas Guy never married. Charitable work in Tamworth and London began early. His good deeds received local recognition but went unrecorded elsewhere and Guy was publicly lampooned as a miserly

74 *Almshouse interior. The living quarters of one of Thomas Guy's almshouses shortly before rebuilding and modernisation in 1913. Ovens are built into the fireplace.*

75 *Weathercock, Town Hall. Decorative wrought iron became fashionable in the early 18th century and enjoyed a creative heyday.*

penny-pincher. The full extent of his philanthropy only began to emerge after his death. Many relatives had received allowances and there were numerous loans to help budding young entrepreneurs start up in business. In 1678, he bought land and opened an almshouse in Tamworth on the site of the former Guildhall at the corner of Gungate and Spinning School Lane. This provided accommodation for seven poor women. Fifteen years later he paid for an extension, doubling the space available and allowing men as well as women to be housed. Occupants had their own entrance and living room. A garden at the rear was used to grow vegetables.

In 1693 the corporation minutes refer to Thomas Guy as 'our incomparable bene-factor' and two years later he was chosen to represent the town in Parliament. In 1701 he footed the bill for a new, purpose-built Town Hall in Market Street, replacing the old Warwickshire hall that had served the town since incorporation. This neat brick and stone building originally had a single large meeting room on the upper storey. Below, a shaded open space between Tuscan columns housed a butter market. At the time the Town Hall was built, decorative wrought iron was becoming fashionable and was about to enjoy a creative heyday. A glazed lantern on the roof carries a weathercock that is a splendid example of the ironsmith's art.

Guy, a Whig before the Whigs became the dominant grouping in the House of Commons, served as the town's parliamentary representative until 1707. When Richard Swinfen was then chosen ahead of him he took rejection as a personal insult and reacted furiously, threatening to demolish the Town

76 *Indenture of election to parliament, 1700. Official confirmation of the return of Sir Henry Gough and Thomas Guy as Members of Parliament for Tamworth, certified by the County Sheriff of Staffordshire.*

77 *Thomas Guy's Charity, trustee donations 1870-6. Corporation minutes refer to Thomas Guy as 'our incomparable benefactor'.*

Hall he had provided. In the end he confined himself to banning residents of the borough from his almshouses. In future only his own needy relatives and inhabitants from surrounding villages were to be allowed entry.

Guy was a governor of St Thomas's Hospital in Southwark and contributed significant sums towards its running costs. St Thomas's specialised as a seamen's hospital and Guy's father had been a lighterman on the Thames. One of his charitable practices was to buy promissory notes issued by the government to sailors during the reign of Charles II instead of wages. He bought notes at a discount of

78 *Thomas Guy's Almshouses, Lower Gungate. After his rejection as their MP in 1707, Thomas Guy reacted by banning residents of the town from his almshouses and restricting entry to 'relatives and hamleteers' only.*

anything up to fifty per cent of face value, but since redemption was uncertain he was buying potentially worthless pieces of paper. Until, that is, they were converted into stocks in the South Sea Company. Nominally set up to offer trading rights with South America, the main aim of the company was to muscle in on the Bank of England and the East India Company, who were jointly administering the national debt. By 1720 the South Sea Company had taken over the whole of the debt, amounting to £31 million. Shareholders collectively covered government borrowing and received an annuity in return. The flaw with the scheme was that the amount of stock linked to each unit of debt was not fixed. It floated according to demand. As long as the price was rising this was not a problem. And rise it did. Speculation fever took hold and the price of stock rocketed, much of it fuelled by unsecured loans taken out by people scrambling for a piece of the action. Thousands were bankrupted when the bubble burst. Thomas Guy was one of the few who read the market and sold before the crash. It has been estimated that Guy's original holding before values soared was in excess of £45,000. This at a time when a labourer in Tamworth could expect to earn between 5d. and 8d. a day, a stonemason or carpenter 1s. a day, and a domestic maid perhaps £1 10s. od. a year 'and found'. Guy's profits enabled the hospital that bears his name to be built on land opposite St Thomas's.

After he died, in 1724, Guy's trustees took out a coat of arms. Exceptionally for a man of humble origins, the award included supporters, two angels who stand either side of the escutcheon or shield, a reflection of the reputation and standing of this remarkable self-made man.

Seven

PROGRESS, POLITICS AND THE PEEL FAMILY

Technological advances in Georgian England created an economic and social revolution. New structural techniques using brick and stone replaced timber framing for houses. Protective lead oxide paints allowed the use of Scandinavian softwood, easy to work and carve, for joinery. Freed from the constraints of the box-frame, architects designed buildings of restrained elegance with symmetrical elevations and tall sash windows. Ornamental emphasis focused on doorways with elaborate porches surrounded by classically inspired pilasters, columns and moulded architraves. Inserting a glass panel above the door to allow natural light into entrance halls became popular in an age of candlelight, when anything remotely resembling a proper window was subject to tax. Decorative semi-circular fanlights (rectangular versions are more properly 'transom lights') glazed with wooden, wrought iron or brass spokes became one of the defining features of the age.

Industrially, textiles, iron and steel, and coal mining led the way. In 1769, just four years after James Hargreaves had invented the spinning jenny, Richard Arkwright patented his water-powered cotton spinning frame. James Watt's steam engine was soon pumping water from deep mine shafts and

79 *Georgian doorway, Aldergate. Building in Georgian England was classically inspired. Ornamental emphasis was reserved for doorways, with decorative fanlights allowing natural light into entrance halls.*

driving machinery. Almost overnight, cotton spinning changed from being a cottage industry into a factory-based operation. Robert Peel, a Lancashire farmer and businessman, was a neighbour of Hargreaves. He quickly recognised the competitive advantage of mass production and mortgaged the family homestead to invest in a textile mill. But not everyone was in favour of progress. Mechanisation threatened hand spinners with the loss of their livelihood. Rioters broke into Peel's premises, destroyed the mill and tossed his new-fangled machines into the River Calder. In 1780, Peel moved his operations to Staffordshire, setting up in Burton upon Trent, where trouble was unlikely and his son had business connections and was in a position to offer suitable sites. It was also close to customers in the East Midlands hosiery business. One of Peel's

printed calico patterns was a single parsley leaf design repeated over a lined background. It became so commercially successful that Peel was nicknamed 'Parsley' Peel.

The new factories needed raw materials, and finished goods had to be transported to markets both domestic and abroad. Inland transport systems were creaking under the strain. Although the River Trent had been made navigable from the east coast as far as Burton upon Trent, and the Corporation actively sought sponsors to extend the navigation within reach of Tamworth, river navigation was slow and uncertain. Improvement was signalled when the country's first long-distance inland waterway, the Trent and Mersey Canal, sponsored by Josiah Wedgwood, the Burslem pottery manufacturer, among others, opened in 1777. Importantly for Robert Peel, the canal

80   *Salters Lane, 1870, approaching Tamworth with St Editha's church in the background. Local roads were deeply rutted and could become impassable after prolonged bad weather.*

81   *Tollhouse, Lady Bridge. Tamworth Turnpike Trust took over all major routes in 1770. Tolls collected from travellers paid for essential maintenance. Only the Royal Mail was exempt from charges. The tollhouse was removed after tolls were lifted in 1883.*

provided Staffordshire with a direct link to Liverpool, where raw cotton was imported. Within a few years the Birmingham and Coventry canals were connected at Fazeley, putting south Staffordshire at the hub of a national waterway network linking the ports on the Humber, Thames, Mersey and Severn estuaries.

Roads had been in decline since the Roman legions marched out. With no over-arching authority for road maintenance, upkeep was a parish responsibility. Tamworth's roads in the middle of the 18th century were deeply rutted. On long journeys three or four more times the numbers of draught animals than were strictly necessary had to be harnessed to haul waggons through the mud and potholes. Ashby Road was particularly bad, turning into an impassable quagmire during wet weather. Before the

Highways Act of 1835 made raising a rate to pay for road maintenance a municipal responsibility, inhabitants were technically required by law to devote a few days direct labour each year to the upkeep of their local byways. In practice the Corporation generally used town funds to pay contractors to undertake the work rather than enforce statute labour. At county level a surveyor of highways had the power to order repairs and claim reimbursement from landowners. It was a highly unsatisfactory state of affairs and the new class of influential industrialists pressed for reform.

Progress came with the setting up of turnpike trusts authorised by private Acts of Parliament. Under this system roads were gated and booths set up to collect tolls. Money raised by charging travellers was reinvested in maintenance. Turnpikes operated on the Ashby and Glascote Roads from 1759. In 1770 Tamworth Turnpike Trust took over all the major routes into the town and instigated a comprehensive scheme of turnpikes. Milestones, not seen since Roman times, were set up at regular intervals. On improved surfaces coaches were able to average up to 10 mph. Journey times were halved. London was now only three days away.

Tolls varied according to the size of vehicle or the number and type of livestock being herded. Rich aristocrats employed 'running footmen' to race ahead and pay the toll to avoid being delayed. Only the Royal Mail was exempt. Tollgate keepers were expected to listen for a distant blast on the posthorn as the mail coach approached and rush out to open the gates so that the vehicle

82 *Milestone, Upper Gungate. This repositioned milestone from the turnpike era is now outside the Health Centre.*

could pass without having to slow down. Mail coaches bound for London, Birmingham and Chester passed through the town daily. Letters were collected from the *King's Arms* and later also from the 18th-century *Castle Hotel*. Both establishments served as posting inns. Until 1784, mounted postboys carried the mail in relays, a dangerous occupation in the heyday of the highwayman. Later, maroon and black mail coaches with red wheels, rims tyred in iron hoops, took over. Post Office guards, young men armed with flintlock pistols and a blunderbuss, were in charge of mail coaches. Guards were supposed to sit outside at the rear of the coach with the mail placed in a locked strongbox beneath their seat. It was still a risky business. Post Office advice issued in 1797 recommended that banknotes or money orders should be cut into two pieces and each half sent separately for security. But the Tamworth mail was only robbed once, and then by a sneak thief who broke into the box while the guard, in breach of the rules, sat up front chatting with the driver. In the second half of the 19th century free-standing pillar boxes and wall-mounted boxes appeared on the streets of the town. By then the railways had taken over the carriage of non-local mail. A post office had opened in Silver Street by 1818, moving shortly afterwards to Church Street and then to Colehill before settling for many years in George Street. By the 1900s a small fleet of postal delivery workers leaving for their rounds astride Royal Mail bicycles was a regular early morning sight.

Passenger coaches called at the *King's Arms* in Market Street and the *George* in George Street. Travellers could catch the *Umpire* for London or Liverpool, the *Original*

83 Castle Hotel, *Lady Bank (c.1872). In the early days of the Royal Mail, letters were collected from posting inns. William Tempest ran the* Castle Hotel *until 1883 and also served as a councillor, mayor and magistrate.*

Prince Coburg between London and Manchester, the *Royal Dart* serving Birmingham and Nottingham, or the *Defiance* on the Birmingham to Sheffield route.

Better road surfaces enabled lighter coaches to be used. Elliptical springs were introduced, ironing out some of the bumps in the road. Local journeys were still made at the pace of a horse. The farmer had his four-wheeled cart and maybe a pony and trap for market; townspeople could hire a horse or a post chaise (advertised in 1818 by James Carter Barton of the *King's Arms* as available

'at a minute's notice'); minor gentry had their gigs, and the Peels, Townshends and Thynnes their phaetons, broughams and racy two-wheeled hansoms with liverymen in full fig. When the ancient market cross in Church Street was removed in the 1850s, the stone steps were recycled to make a mounting block – a set of steps often found outside local hostelries to help patrons into the saddle. Trade was sufficient to support a number of saddlers, wheelwrights and blacksmiths in the town. With competition from the railway, long-distance horse-drawn coach services

84 *Postal workers, George Street (1900). A small fleet of delivery staff leaving for their rounds astride Royal Mail bicycles was once a familiar early morning sight.*

were soon superseded. Traffic reduced to a point that made the turnpikes unprofitable. In 1883 the Turnpike Trust was wound up, all local roads were freed from tolls and responsibility for their maintenance passed to the corporation and county authorities. In 1891 a highways department depot was built in Salters Lane.

In 1795, severe winter weather and floods swept away two of Lady Bridge's 12 medieval arches. Pointed Gothic arches were require more supporting piers than semi-circular vaulting, and as a result, they are subjected to increased scouring in the restricted current. Lady Bridge was rebuilt in its present six-arched form the following year. The River Tame marked the town limits and the cost was shared equally by the Corporation and Staffordshire County authorities. Increasing use caused problems of congestion at the crossing and led to Sir Robert Peel contributing most of the funding necessary for widening the approaches to allow two-way traffic.

Bole Bridge, with pedestrian refuges above triangular cutwaters, was an equally narrow bottleneck. The medieval bridge was eventually replaced in 1877.

In 1808, the town streets were flagged and kerbstones laid to make proper pedestrian pavements. By 1839, the recently formed Tamworth Gaslight and Coke Company were

85 *Anker Viaduct. George Stephenson, self-educated inventor of the first practical railway engines, himself drove the first locomotive,* Tamworth, *across the 250m. long viaduct above the River Anker in 1839, pulling six carriages filled with local dignitaries invited to mark the event.*

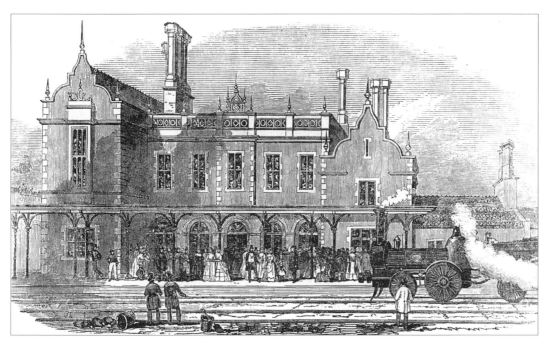

86 *Railway station, 1847, built in time for the opening of the London and North Western Railway's Trent Valley line linking Tamworth to Stafford and the north west and, via Rugby, to London.*

providing street lighting from their works at the lower end of Bolebridge Street.

In 1839, the Birmingham and Derby Junction Railway laid tracks through the town, crossing the Anker Valley on a 250m. viaduct. George Stephenson himself drove the first locomotive, *Tamworth* across its 19 arches. An imposing station in Jacobean style with tall decorative chimneys was built in time for the opening of the London and North Western Railway's Trent Valley Line in 1847, linking the town to Stafford and the north-west, and via Rugby, with London.

Robert Peel: Industrialist (1st Baronet)

It was partly improved transport links that persuaded 'Parsley' Peel's son Robert to build cotton mills at Tamworth, Fazeley and Bonehill. Young Robert Peel had made his

money as a partner in the Bury mills belonging to his uncle, Jonathan Howarth, and his future father-in-law, William Yates. Howarth and Yates had been in business with his father. As they retired from active management Robert took more and more control until eventually he was in sole charge.

Lady Meadow was the site of Peel's first mills in 1788. Then Castle Mill, a complex of three corn mills and a fulling mill, was adapted for cotton production. Fulling, a process in which wool was scoured then felted by pounding with hammers, was in decline by the end of the 18th century, replaced by worsted cloth spun from a twisted yarn of combed wool. A hard-wearing worsted of the time popular with working women was known colloquially as 'tammy', supposedly from its manufacture in

87   *Drayton Manor. Robert Peel purchased the Drayton Estate in 1796 and commissioned leading architect Robert Smirke to design a magnificent house.*

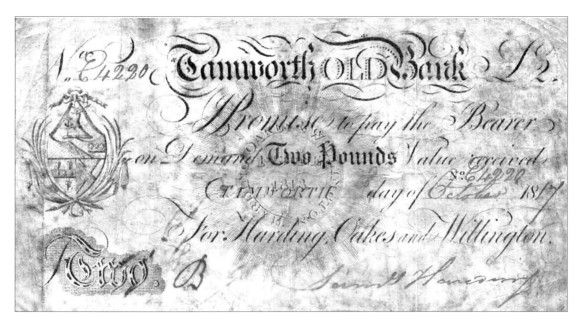

88   *Tamworth banknote. A two-pound note issued by Tamworth Old Bank of Harding, Oakes and Willington in 1817. The bank crashed in 1819. Until Sir Robert Peel put the Bank of England in charge of regulating the issue of paper money in 1844, many banks issued their own, each note individually numbered, dated and signed.*

Tamworth. Peel rented the Banqueting Hall of the castle for use as a forge. Textiles soon overtook tanning as the principal industry of the town. It was mainly women and children, some as young as seven years, who were employed at the mills, often working from 6a.m. to 9p.m. with a one-hour break for dinner and recreation.

Peel moved permanently from Lancashire to Drayton Bassett, completing the purchase of the Drayton estates from the Thynne family in 1796. Celebrated architect Robert Smirke was commissioned to draw up plans for a magnificent new house, Drayton Manor. Equally renowned garden designer William Gilpin was chosen to landscape the grounds.

Peel was elected Member of Parliament for the town in 1790 and served continuously until 1820, becoming a baronet in 1800. He used his parliamentary influence to improve conditions in factories. His advocacy helped the passage of the Health and Morals of Apprentices Act (1802), which placed limits on the hours that could be worked by pauper children sent as parish apprentices and ensured they received clothing and basic education. When Peel gave evidence to a select committee investigating the conditions of children in the factories he explained that his many business interests prevented him from visiting his mills very often. However, he did admit, 'Whenever such visits were made, I was struck with the uniform appearance of bad health, and in many cases, stunted growth of the children.' Peel retired from the cotton business in 1818 a multi-millionaire. His support helped the passage of the Factory Act (1819), banning the employment of children below the age of nine years.

Early Banking

Robert Peel was commercially active in the area before beginning textile production. The new industrial economy needed finance and many wealthy businessmen were becoming involved in oiling the wheels. In the late 1770s Peel and his partner Joseph Wilkes opened a bank in Tamworth.

Joseph Wilkes was an entrepreneur from Overseal in south Derbyshire who had his finger in many business pies. As well as being a banker, Wilkes was a director of the company that leased navigation rights on the River Trent and also had interests in brick making, coal mining, boat building and farming. He had provided land for 'Parsley' Peel's mills at Burton upon Trent and cut the channels to supply them with water power. Robert Peel had been involved with a bank in Manchester and became Wilkes's partner in the Tamworth venture. It was Wilkes's capital that enabled the initial purchase of the Drayton Estate from Sir Thomas Thynne.

89   *Bank House, Holloway, from 1845 the home of Tamworth Savings Bank, founded in 1823 by Sir Robert Peel in the wake of a commercial banking crisis in the town. The bank opened for just one hour each week and operated until 1897.*

Paper currency with a face value far in excess of its intrinsic worth was still a relatively new idea. By the time Peel and Wilkes opened their establishment, banks in London had abandoned the practice of printing their own banknotes in favour of Bank of England stock. Provincial banks were still issuing notes under their own name secured on the bank's capital deposits.

In 1790, Peel and Wilkes expanded into the capital's finance market, merging with Dickenson and Goodall of Poultry, London. Peel appears to have stepped down soon after and Wilkes's son-in-law, the Reverend Thomas Fisher, took his place.

Two new banks now set up in town. Paget and Corgan, and the Tamworth Old Bank run by three partners, Harding, Oakes and Willington. Both local banks initially drew on Wilkes and Company in London. Problems arose after the end of the Napoleonic Wars in 1815. Nationally, the war had generated profits for many businesses and provided employment. Once it was over discharged servicemen flooded the labour market, unemployment rose, prices fell and recession followed. Paget and Corgan failed in 1816, the market got the jitters and Tamworth Old Bank, unable to withstand a sustained run on its deposits, crashed in 1819. Many residents found themselves out of pocket. Small businesses and traders were particularly hard hit.

Sir Robert Peel partially plugged the gap left by the demise of the commercial banks by founding Tamworth Savings Bank in 1823. Within a short time it had attracted deposits in excess of £18,000 from 529 individual savers and charitable groups. Although the Savings Bank was only open for one hour each week, from noon till 1p.m. on Mondays, it was successful and operated until 1897.

There was still a need for a commercial bank, but confidence was not restored when a branch opened by Northern and Central Bank in 1834 lasted only two years. It was taken over by the Lichfield, Rugeley and Tamworth Bank but they too soon ran into trouble. To avert another crash and to protect its local interests, the National Provincial Bank, one of a new breed of national banks founded on the joint stock principles that preceded the notion of limited liability, opened negotiations with the Lichfield, Rugeley and Tamworth company. Winding up was a protracted business. Debts and defaults took years to settle but the National Provincial's intervention saved the day. Other large national banks followed them into the town. Financial stability was underpinned by the Bank Charter Act of 1844, passed when Sir Robert Peel, the 2nd Baronet, was Prime Minister. Among a raft of regulations introduced to protect the public's money was a restriction on the issue of local banknotes.

Robert Peel: Statesman (2nd Baronet)

When Robert Peel was born in 1788, his father reportedly pledged his son to serve his country. He entered Parliament at the age of 21 years, representing Cashel in Ireland, and remained a member of the House of Commons for the rest of his life. Following the death of his father in 1830, he represented Tamworth.

Peel's parliamentary rise was rapid. Junior minister, Under Secretary for War and the Colonies, then Secretary for Ireland before becoming an outstanding Home Secretary.

90   *Sir Robert Peel, 2nd Baronet (1788-1850). When the future Prime Minister was born his father is reputed to have pledged his son to serve his country. Peel entered Parliament at the age of 21 years and remained a member of the House of Commons for the rest of his life.*

At the Home Office he reformed an antiquated legal system and founded the Metropolitan Police to take over from professional thief-takers, the watch and local constables. Members of the new force were soon nicknamed 'bobbies' or 'peelers' in his honour. The Municipal Corporations Act (1835) called upon boroughs to set up their own forces on a similar pattern.

Defeat for the Tories in their long-running opposition to Whig proposals for electoral reform had split and damaged the party. Finally passed in 1832, the Reform Act abolished 'rotten boroughs', where a single landowner might control the seat, and redistributed those available. At Tamworth, the parliamentary borough boundaries were extended in line with the ecclesiastical parish, bringing Amington, Bolehall, Comberford, Fazeley, Glascote, Hopwas, Wigginton and Wilnecote into the enlarged constituency. The Reform Act also lowered the property value at which householders qualified for the vote. Measures increased the total electorate by more than 50 per cent but it was still only the relatively prosperous middle class who went to the polls.

William IV became the last monarch to exercise the royal prerogative and dismiss his Prime Minister against the wishes of Parliament, dismissing Lord Melbourne and sending for Peel. Peel responded to the King's call and the needs of his party with the Tamworth Manifesto, a pioneering election address sent to every voter in the town and carried by all the national newspapers. In it Peel set out the principles that would inform an administration under his leadership. He pledged to accept the changes introduced by the Reform Act and acknowledged the need to tackle social inequality, proposing a 'middle way' of moderate change that balanced the needs of all sections of society. It was a political project, an attempt to reinvent the old Tory Party as new Conservatives. But there was little time to implement his ideas. Within a few months electoral defeat returned the Whigs to power and Lord Melbourne was back at the helm.

After the death of William, Queen Consort Adelaide came to stay at Drayton Manor. In 1843, Queen Victoria and Prince Albert visited and crowds lined the streets to catch a glimpse of the royal couple. The following year Czar Nicholas I was Peel's guest.

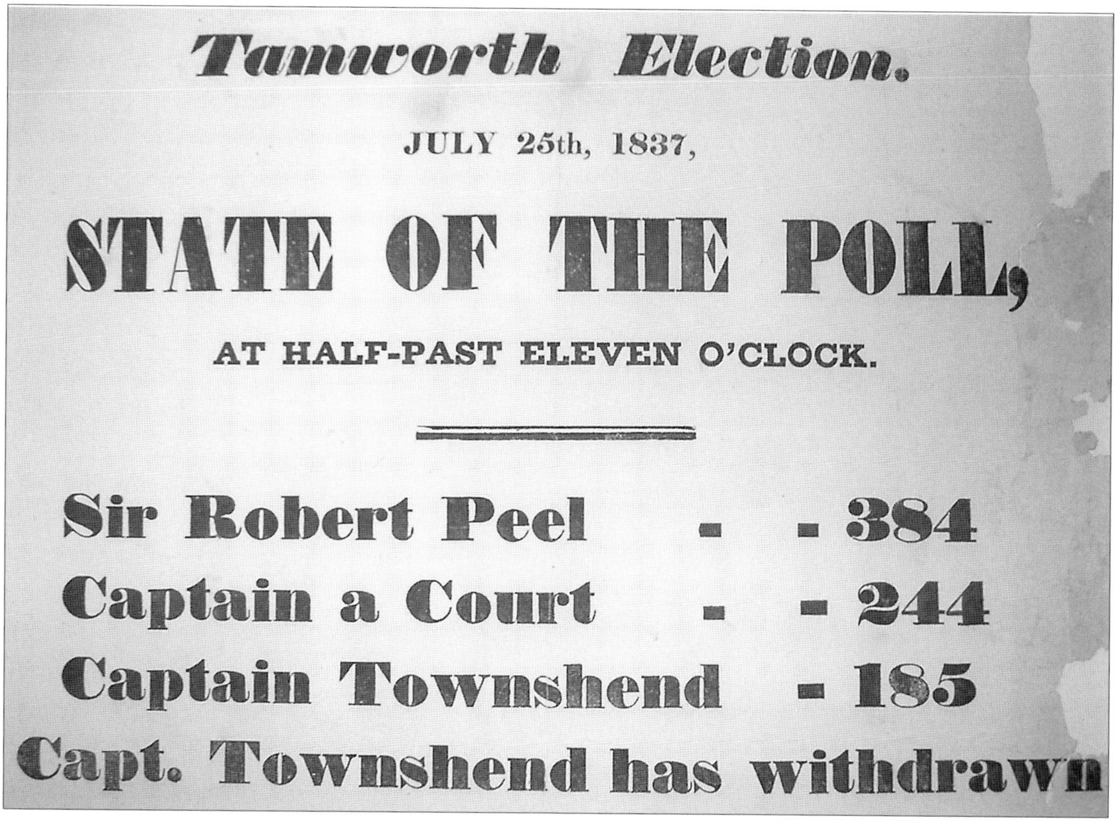

Tamworth Election.

JULY 25th, 1837,

STATE OF THE POLL,

AT HALF-PAST ELEVEN O'CLOCK.

Sir Robert Peel · · 384
Captain a Court · · 244
Captain Townshend · 185
Capt. Townshend has withdrawn

91 *State of the Poll, 1837. Details of the parliamentary election of 29 June, sitting members Sir Robert Peel and Captain Edward à Court comfortably retaining their seats ahead of Captain John Townshend.*

The young Queen Victoria had depended heavily on Lord Melbourne. When Peel became Prime Minister for a second time in 1841 she thought his manner distant, and it was some time before he won her confidence. Peel's energy and abilities characterised a progressive and competent administration. He personally supervised the work of every government department. Under his prudent leadership a stagnant economy revived. A cautious reformer, he gradually became a convert to the idea of free trade. Customs duties and import tariffs were reviewed and reduced, but the protectionist Corn Laws posed a problem. Landowners had a vested interest in maintaining artificially high prices but Peel's Whig opponents had the support of many in his own party. Angry demonstrations took place at home. The potato famine in Ireland led to even more disaffection and violence. Peel faced a dilemma. In pushing through repeal of the Corn Laws for the greater good of the nation he knew he was splitting the Conservative Party and putting his political future on the line. Peel announced his decision, to revoke the Corn Laws and allow cheap imports, from the window of the Town Hall in Tamworth. In Parliament he won the crucial vote to secure the passage of his proposals but lost

TO THE ELECTORS

OF THE

BOROUGH OF TAMWORTH.

GENTLEMEN,

On the 26th of November last, being then at Rome, I received from his Majesty a summons, wholly unforeseen and unexpected by me, to return to England without delay, for the purpose of assisting his Majesty in the formation of a new Government. I instantly obeyed the command for my return, and, on my arrival, I did not hesitate, after an anxious review of the position of public affairs, to place at the disposal of my Sovereign any services which I might be thought capable of rendering.

B 2

VISIT OF HER MOST GRACIOUS MAJESTY

QUEEN VICTORIA,

AND

HIS ROYAL HIGHNESS PRINCE ALBERT,

TO TAMWORTH,

ON TUESDAY, THE 28th DAY OF NOVEMBER, 1843.

NOTICE

Her Majesty will proceed from the Railway along the Station Road, George Street, Market Street, and by way of Bonehill to Drayton Manor.

No Carriages or Horses, except those of the Royal Escort will be permitted to enter upon the Station Road during the day, until after Her Majesty has passed. No Carriages or Horses will be allowed to cross from Bolebridge Street to Colehill, after half-past Two o'Clock, and no Carriages or Horses will be allowed to enter into George Street, or Market Street after One o'Clock. No Carriages or Horsemen to remain stationary in Silver Street, the Holloway, or on the Road to Lady Bridge after Two o'Clock. No Carriages or Horses, except those of the Royal Escort, will be permitted to stand upon the Road between Lady Bridge and Bonehill, after Two o'Clock; and the public are therefore requested to take their Stations in the Fields adjoining the Road, the occupiers of which have kindly consented to allow them to do so.

No foot passengers will be allowed to occupy the centre of the Streets or Roads through which Her Majesty passes.

The Committee particularly request the attention of the Public to the above arrangements, that order may be preserved and accidents avoided.

ROYAL BLUE FAVOURS WILL BE WORN, AND THE MEMBERS OF THE COMMITTEE WILL BE DISTINGUISHED BY A ROSETTE ON THE LEFT ARM.

92 & 93   *Tamworth Manifesto, introduction. All the national newspapers carried Sir Robert Peel's pioneering political address to the voters of Tamworth in 1834. The document signalled the emergence of the Conservative Party and is widely accepted as the forerunner of all modern election manifestos; and notice of visit by Queen Victoria and Prince Albert. Crowds lined the streets to catch a glimpse of the royal couple when they came to stay at Drayton Manor as guests of Sir Robert Peel.*

too much support in the process. His dominance of the political stage was over and he resigned in 1846.

Four years later Peel was thrown from his horse on London's Constitution Hill and died from the injuries he sustained. Instead of the expected state funeral at Westminster Abbey his family chose a more private service.

His body was brought back to Drayton Bassett for burial at tiny St Peter's church. An ornamental marble canopy caps a simple memorial tablet on the north wall of the church. Public subscriptions paid for a bronze statue by Matthew Noble to be erected outside the old Town Hall in Market Street which was unveiled in 1852.

Eight

VICTORIAN VALUES: TRADE, HEALTH AND EDUCATION

In 1835 the Municipal Corporations Act replaced the bailiffs and capital burgesses with a corporate body of 12 councillors, directly elected by the ratepayers, and four aldermen. Robert Nevill took up office as mayor on 1 January 1836. Meetings continued to be held in the Town Hall in Market Street, with the rooms in the extension enlarged to accommodate various committees set up to plan and carry out the duties of the new authority.

The requirement for traders to be admitted as freemen of the borough in order to transact business in the town was officially abolished. In practice this had long since quietly lapsed. Honorary freedom was introduced as a way of recognising out-standing contributions to civic life but it was 1951 before the first admission. Sir Robert Peel, the current incumbent, made an unsuccessful plea for the honorary position of high steward to be retained.

A single cell beneath the Town Hall was insufficient for a fully functioning local justice system. When a small police station was set up in Church Street it had two holding cells but it was more cost effective to send prisoners charged with criminal offences to the gaol at Stafford for trial at the county court. The Court of Record, the old portmanmoot court, had not met since 1792 and was wound up. The Court Leet and Court Baron had merged in 1750. After 1836 sessions were restricted to occasional civic purposes and the court met for the last time in 1876. Subsequently all functions were transferred to the county court.

Industry in the area was revitalised in the middle of the 19th century following a brief period of stagnation after Robert Peel (1st Baronet) had sold his mills and retired. Under the ownership of men like Charles Harding of the Bolehall Mill Company, William Tolson at Fazeley and Etienne Bruno Hamel, the textile mills began to prosper again.

William Tolson bought the Fazeley mill from Peel in 1843. His sons expanded the business, kept pace with technical innovation and built a new steam-driven operation that doubled capacity. At its peak, some four hundred looms clattered in Tolson's Mill. Huge quantities of tape and webbing were produced for binding carpets and trimming corsets, dresses and a whole range of fashionable clothing.

Bruno Hamel had fled the 'Terror' of the French Revolution, escaping from con-finement in Dieppe Castle, after hearing that both his parents had been sent to the guillotine. He established himself in

94   *Freedom of the borough certificate. The requirement for those wanting to conduct business in the town to become freemen of the borough had not been applied for many years when it was officially abolished in 1835. Honorary freedom was introduced as a way of recognising outstanding service to the community. The first recipient was Alderman Frederick Allton JP in 1951.*

Tamworth as a French teacher, married local girl Elizabeth Hunter and opened a small business in Market Street dealing in china, glass and earthenware. His son Etienne Bruno was born in 1796, married Elizabeth Pierce in 1822 and worked as an artist, producing a series of illustrations of Tamworth that have been much reproduced since they first appeared in 1829. Help from the Peel family, then winding down their involvement in textile manufacture, enabled the Hamels to get into the business. They bought a large house in Bolebridge Street, installed a homemade loom and began manufacturing tape in 1837. The mill flourished under successive generations, supplying government offices with the 'red tape' for documents, which has become synonymous with rigid official formality, and the armed services with webbing.

In 1869, Thomas Cooke took a 21-year lease on the castle. From small beginnings Cooke had built up a successful wholesale clothing business, moving to a factory in Lichfield Street that was eventually bought by John Shannon and Sons of Walsall in 1904. Thomas Cooke junior married Frances, only daughter of Etienne Bruno Hamel. A joint Cooke/Hamel clothing factory venture at Kettlebrook was later sold to Bradleys of Chester.

Castle Mill and Alders Mill were converted to produce paper from rag pulp as well as continuing in part to grind corn. Castle Mills declined and had ceased to operate by the close of the 19th century. Messrs Fowler at Alders Mill were declared bankrupt in 1828. Eventually Alders was taken over by Charles Fisher, who began printing wallpaper by automated process, later moving to

95 *William Tolson's Mill, Fazeley. Formerly owned by Peel and bought by Tolson in 1843, this is now converted into an enterprise park housing a variety of small businesses.*

Kettlebrook Mill where the business ran until the 1930s. Alders passed through the hands of a couple of owners before becoming Alders (Tamworth) Limited, who enlarged the works.

In 1848, the first deep shafts were sunk at Pooley Hall Colliery. Coal mining became a major industry and flourished for over a century. Clay quarries also exploited the area's rich natural resources. In 1847, John Gibbs teamed up with colliery owner Charles Canning to manufacture bricks, tiles and stoneware at works in Glascote. Sinks and drainage pipes were the main business but

96 *Etienne Bruno Hamel (1824-95), son of Etienne Bruno Hamel the artist, married Mary Shaw in 1845 and helped expand the family's narrow fabric manufacturing business.*

97 *Alders Mill, number 2 papermaking machine with rollers, calendars and winding reel. Four centuries of papermaking in Tamworth came to end with the closure of Alders in 1993.*

98 *Pooley Hall Colliery, royal visit. The first deep shafts were sunk in 1848. The future King George VI (then Duke of York) visited the mine in 1924.*

99   *Caryatid by Gibbs and Canning. Individual decorative architectural pieces from the Glascote factory were in demand worldwide. This caryatid was bound for Vancouver, Canada.*

100   *Long-case clock in the state withdrawing room at Tamworth Castle, made about 1860 by local craftsman William Lakin of Market Street. The clock face is hand painted and was re-glazed in 1998.*

designers and architects worldwide were soon commissioning individual decorative architectural pieces. By 1900 Gibbs and Canning employed around three hundred people. Among other London landmarks, their work decorated the *Savoy Hotel*, the Royal Albert Hall and the Natural History Museum. Chief modeller in the early 20th century, Mr M. Latchford, trained at the Royal College of Art in London.

Small businesses too thrived in a largely self-sufficient town. A population of a little over four thousand in the 1850s was served by a wide range of trades, crafts and professions, including numerous bakers, butchers and even a couple of candlestick makers (tallow chandlers). The former Union Workhouse in Lady Bank was taken over by Mr E. Morgan of the *Castle Hotel* and became Castle Brewery. Drinkers had a choice of twenty-five or so public houses. A tradition of watch and clockmaking begun by Henry Tristram at 13 George Street during the first half of the 18th century expanded after railway timetables and factory work made accurate timekeeping a necessity. Among those who followed in Tristram's footsteps, the best remembered names are those of William Lakin, Charles Pickering and George Griffin. But it was not an all-male preserve. Ann Baker of Market Street built up a considerable reputation in the trade.

In 1867, a monthly cattle market began. After six years of sales in Church Street a livestock yard opened in Victoria Road. Fortnightly auctions were held on alternate Mondays and a café was added.

101 *Russian anchor, Castle Grounds, a trophy from the Crimean War brought originally to Drayton Manor by William Peel, third son of Sir Robert Peel (2nd Baronet). In 1849, at the age of 24, he became the youngest captain in the Royal Navy and in 1857 was one of the first recipients of the Victoria Cross.*

Before the Corporation took over responsibility in 1871, volunteers ran a local fire service. They were unable to prevent the deaths of six women servants trapped by a fire in their top-storey bedroom at the *Castle Hotel* in 1838. At a memorial service held for the women at St Editha's church, the Reverend Dickenson said the origin of the fire remained a complete mystery. After the disaster, permission was given to store the fire tender between the arches below the Town Hall and for one of the Corporation's horses to pull the apparatus.

An obelisk in the churchyard of St Editha's commemorates the tragedy at the *Castle Hotel*. A second obelisk nearby is a memorial to Edward Farmer (1809-76), who lived in Tamworth for many years. Farmer, a detective with the railway, was a writer who specialised in tragic tales in which children often suffered bravely before expiring in their mother's arms. His best known work, *Little Jim*, set in Polesworth, is a typically melodramatic tearjerker ('I have no pain, dear mother, now; But oh! I am so dry: Just moisten poor Jim's lips once more; And, mother, do not cry!'). It was a popular party piece recited in many Victorian parlours.

There was a tragic railway accident in the early hours of 14 September 1870. The Irish Mail, *en route* to London from Holyhead, was mistaken for a late running goods train. Preparations to shunt the expected goods train off the main track led the express onto a siding at full speed. The locomotive ploughed through the buffers, left the rails and plummeted into the River Anker. Amazingly the death toll was limited to the driver, fireman and one passenger, a priest.

Politically, the Peels and the Townshends continued to exert their influence. When Sir Robert Peel died in 1850, his eldest son Robert, then aged 28, came into property amounting to around a third of the town. Younger son William joined the Royal Navy as a midshipman at the age of 13 and served with distinction in the Crimean War as captain of the frigate *Diamond*. He returned from Russia with an anchor captured from an enemy ship before leaving Drayton Manor for the last time bound for India in command of the *Shannon*. He was wounded taking part in the second relief of Lucknow during the Indian Mutiny, caught smallpox and died at Cawnpore in 1858.

Robert took over his father's seat as Member of Parliament for Tamworth. In 1856, he married Lady Emily Hay. Dr John Woody of the Moat House paid for the bells of St Editha's to be rung over two days to celebrate the happy occasion. Emily became Robert's partner in folly as the couple embarked on a spree of spectacular gambling compounded by frivolous litigation that left them bankrupt within two decades.

Sir Robert's love of the turf prompted him to start his own stud at Bonehill, where his horses lived in better conditions than many people. Spacious stables were lit and heated by gas. Occasional race meetings had been held on Staffordshire Moor. With sponsorship from Peel, the first properly organised meeting took place on Calford Meadow at Easter 1865. Opposition from the more strait-laced inhabitants of the town intensified after a specially erected grandstand collapsed killing one spectator and injuring many others. Objectors were

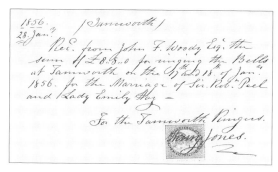

102 *Receipt for bell ringing. Dr John Woody of the Moat House paid for the bells of St Editha's to be rung over two days in 1856 to celebrate the wedding of Sir Robert Peel (3rd Baronet) to Lady Emily Hay.*

103 *Petition in favour of the Easter races. The first properly organised horse races on Staffordshire Moor, sponsored by Sir Robert Peel (3rd Baronet), were held on Easter Monday 1865. Opposition grew after the grandstand collapsed in 1866, killing one spectator and injuring many others. This 1868 petition gathered 92 signatures in support. The meeting became an annual event for many years.*

countered in 1868 by a petition in support of the event signed by 92 householders. For many years the races were an annual event.

Sir Robert's unpredictable behaviour and intemperate lifestyle led to unpopularity. In a bitter electoral dogfight for the second Tamworth seat in 1868, Sir Robert brought in Sir Henry Bulwer-Lytton to challenge distant relative John Peel, a Manchester businessman now living at Middleton Hall. Accusations of corruption and attempts to rig the vote led to charges against Sir Robert and his agent, former alderman John Carmichael. Although Sir Robert was cleared and awarded costs, his reputation was further tarnished.

In the same year as the election fiasco, the Peel School was forced to close temporarily while the Charity Commissioners investigated a £6,000 hole in the accounts that Sir Robert, the sole trustee, was unable to explain. Three years later, and desperate for cash, Sir Robert sold the bulk of a collection of fine paintings to the National Gallery. Mostly acquired by his grandfather, the works included masterpieces by Van Dyck and Rubens among others. By now, Drayton Manor was in the hands of trustees. From 1884 the Peel Estate began to be broken up and sold off piecemeal to pay an increasing list of creditors. In 1893, Peel's daughter Nellie escaped for a while to take the trip of a lifetime aboard a yacht accompanying the convoy delivering track for the Trans-Siberian Railway, becoming accredited in the process

104 & 105 *Election poster, 1868. Sir Robert Peel (3rd Baronet) was accused of bribery and vote rigging in the run up to an election that turned into a mudslinging match between Peel's candidate, Sir Henry Bulwer-Lytton, and John Peel of Middleton Hall, of whom both were fighting the second of Tamworth's parliamentary seats; and Anti-Peel squib, 1868. This satirical notice appeared after the Peel School closed pending investigation by the Charity Commissioners into missing cash. Frederick Ruffe was the mayor and had acted as Peel's treasurer.*

106 *The gallery, Drayton Manor. A collection of fine paintings acquired by the 1st Baronet was sold in 1871 by his grandson in desperate need of money to fund an increasingly profligate lifestyle.*

as the first Englishwoman to walk within the Arctic Circle. Two years later her brother, Sir Robert (4th Baronet), inherited the family debts and proceeded to add to them. His father's stud was sold and more heirlooms were despatched to the salerooms in an attempt to maintain a lifestyle which involved mixing with the Prince of Wales's inner circle. Before marrying Swiss aristocrat Mercedes von Graffenreid, Sir Robert's name was linked romantically with music hall star Lillie Langtry.

In 1889 Tamworth's historic division between Staffordshire and Warwickshire was ended. New county responsibilities introduced by the 1888 Local Government Act made the split unworkable. According to the 1881 census, Staffordshire Tamworth had the larger population and so the Warwickshire side transferred. A year later the municipal boundary was extended eastwards to the railway line, taking in part of the parishes of Bolehall and Glascote, significantly increasing the size of the town. For electoral purposes Tamworth remained a town of two halves although direct parliamentary representation ended in 1895. The Staffordshire seat was subsumed in a new Lichfield division and that for Warwickshire in an enlarged Tamworth division covering north Warwickshire. When constituencies were redrawn in 1918 the boundary was moved to assign Tamworth entirely to Staffordshire.

Health and Welfare

Despite the growth and vitality of early Victorian Tamworth, in the middle of the 19th century it was still a relatively poor and backward town. Mortality rates were high and poverty at such a level that the Poor Rate rose to eight shillings in the pound.

While forward-looking towns elsewhere were tackling public health issues and installing sewage and drainage systems, in Tamworth open gutters ran down the streets. Effluent was discharged directly into the Tame, polluting the river and the water supply. Anyone expecting the municipal reforms of 1835 to bring about sweeping changes was soon disillusioned. The representation had been broadened but it was the same penny-pinching clique of small businessmen holding the reins. Mayor Robert Nevill, a solicitor, was a former bailiff and the new council and aldermen were drawn from the same narrow group of local dignitaries.

The Council took a blinkered view of their welfare responsibilities, pronouncing public health no worse than in other similar towns. They had a point; few small market towns had a piped water supply much before the 1890s and many townspeople objected to the expense of installation. Meetings were held and a local Board of Health was formed, but nothing practical happened as a result, prompting a spate of satirical notices accusing the Council of hypocrisy. Individual members of a committee formed to promote a sewage and waterworks scheme were lampooned as 'the limping old knacker' and 'chat a no go' by opponents. Backers of the proposals circulated a petition, gathering a large number of signatures in support. Campaigners met with a steadfast refusal to increase the rate burden to fund a programme of investment in civic improvements. It took the crusading efforts of radical vicars, Brooke Lambert and William MacGregor, to shake the Council out of its complacency and bring about a change in attitude.

The Cottage Hospital envisaged by Lambert and funded by MacGregor opened with six beds in 1880. Matron Clarke, who trained under Florence Nightingale, was the sole nurse. A dispensary was attached where townspeople could have prescriptions filled in return for paying an annual membership fee. Demand soon led to an expansion of services; public subscriptions paid for an extension at the hospital. A new wing was added in 1889 by Elizabeth Hutton of Dosthill Hall in memory of her husband, Michael, a former manager at Charles Fisher's Mill. In 1892 an Isolation Hospital was built at Bolehall on the edge of Warwickshire Moor to handle infectious diseases, and a joint hospital board was set up. In 1903 work began on building St Editha's Hospital on land between Comberford Road and Wigginton Road.

Water mains were finally laid in 1881. Fresh water was piped from a reservoir at Glascote supplied from a deep well at Hopwas. Conditions were still too slow to improve for many. A few years after the provision of mains water, the Reverend MacGregor noted 23 tenants of five houses sharing a single water closet.

Laying the mains enabled MacGregor to open his indoor public baths in Church Street in 1885. Water in the pool was changed twice a week. Swimmers were charged extra to bathe when the water was fresh.

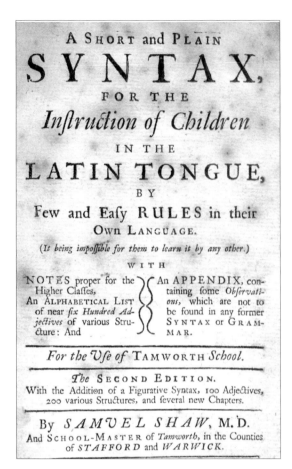

A SHORT and PLAIN

SYNTAX,

FOR THE

Inftruction of Children

IN THE

LATIN TONGUE,

BY

Few and Eafy RULES in their
Own LANGUAGE.

(It being impoffible for them to learn it by any other.)

WITH

NOTES proper for the } { An APPENDIX, con-
Higher Claffes, } { taining fome *Obfervati-*
An ALPHABETICAL LIST } { *ons*, which are not to
of near *fix Hundred Ad-* } { be found in any former
jectives of various Stru- } { SYNTAX or GRAM-
cture: And } { MAR.

For the Ufe of TAMWORTH School.

The SECOND EDITION.
With the Addition of a Figurative Syntax, 100 Adjectives,
200 various Structures, and feveral new Chapters.

By *SAMVEL SHAW*, M.D.
And SCHOOL-MASTER of *Tamworth*, in the Counties
of *STAFFORD* and *WARWICK.*

107 *Samuel Shaw's* Syntax. *Lessons at the grammar school concentrated on the classics. Dr Shaw, schoolmaster from 1709-30, wrote his own Latin textbook for use by students.*

In 1898, Elizabeth Hutton gave the town what became for many years a familiar landmark. The Fountain, on a grassy triangle known as the 'hand', the site of the former town gallows where Upper Gungate meets the Ashby, Comberford and Wigginton roads, provided fresh drinking water for people, horses, dogs and livestock. Three troughs were set around a plinth carrying a five-metre-high granite column with an octagonal copper lantern on top. Brass cups attached by chains were supplied for thirsty travellers.

Education

Until the Victorian concept of moral improvement for the working classes took hold education was limited. Most children did not go to school. Half the population grew up unable to read or write. Schooling was available mainly to boys of a privileged background. The grammar school in Lower Gungate was no exception. Queen Elizabeth's Charter of 1588 made the members of the Corporation governors of the school. Lessons concentrated on the Classics – Greek, Latin and English being taught. Schoolmasters were appointed for life, directly linking the success of the school to the quality and abilities of the persons selected. Under a series of shrewd appointments, perhaps most notably George Antrobus, who was in post for 49 years from 1659 until 1708, and his successor, Dr Samuel Shaw, the school thrived. It began to go downhill after 1805 at the hands of an unsatisfactory master. The Reverend Charles Collins eventually resigned in 1813 and for a few months the school was closed. It was decided that all future contracts of employment should include provision for six months' notice to be given.

As the grammar school struggled, the trustees of John Rawlett's charity increased the number of places available under the terms of his 1686 bequest. Rooms in Church Street were used to provide 12 places to prepare boys for apprenticeship, and ten girls were taught to read and sew. It was still not enough to meet the needs of a growing population and in 1820 Sir Robert Peel the industrialist took over the Church Street schoolrooms and established a free school with room for 100 boys. His son, the 2nd

108 & 109   *George Townshend, 3rd Marquis (1778-1855). Scandal accompanied the breakdown of his marriage to Jane Dunn Gardiner; and Lady Jane Townshend. After leaving her husband Lady Jane contracted a second bigamous marriage but claimed the child born soon afterwards was the son and heir of George Townshend.*

Baronet, moved the school to 17 Lichfield Street in 1837 and then had larger premises built opposite in 1850. Peel commissioned Sydney Smirke to design the new school, a neat brick building with a small playground attached. Sydney was the younger brother of Robert Smirke, the architect who had worked on the plans for Drayton Manor.

Andrew Bell, an army chaplain, developed new ideas on teaching. His approach involved training the most able pupils to teach others. Bell published a pamphlet entitled *Sketch of a National Institution* in 1808 outlining his concept. With large classes and a shortage of teachers his method, known as the monitorial system, attracted considerable attention. He

formed the National Society for Promoting the Education of the Poor in the Principles of the Established Church. With influential support from nationally known figures such as William Wordsworth and Robert Southey, a movement to establish National Schools across the country grew rapidly. Church-sponsored fund-raising activities led by the Reverend Francis Blick, who had been tutor to the young Sir Robert Peel, helped to open a National School in College Lane in 1828. Bible classes were held on Sundays. Lessons during the rest of the week focused on 'the three R's', with additional needlework classes for girls. Children learned by reciting and copying onto chalk and slate boards.

As the number of places available locally increased, an element of choice and competition was introduced into education for the first time; the grammar school suffered. In 1823, there were only four students and they received just two hours of Latin tuition each morning before attending lessons elsewhere. In 1826, the recently introduced notice clause in the master's contract was nearly invoked when the Reverend Samuel Downes received a warning letter about his poor performance. In the event he chose to resign rather than face the ignominy of dismissal.

Governorship of the grammar school transferred from the councillors to trustees following municipal reform in 1835. There were signs of improvement but by now the buildings were in a dilapidated condition. In 1863, the trustees decided urgent action was necessary. Plans were advanced for a new school and an appeal for public contributions was launched. The old premises were sold and replaced by a new grammar school that opened in 1868 at the junction of Upper Gungate and Ashby Road. Students were charged fees to attend the new school, with 12 places set aside for scholarship students.

The pace of change in education was increasing. A wider range of subjects became available including geography, science and practical topics such as woodwork and cookery. The Education Act of 1870 made schooling compulsory for children from the ages of five to 13 years. Lessons were usually from 9a.m. to 5p.m. with a break at midday of two hours. A school attached to St John's opened for the children of Roman Catholic families. An independent School Board formed in 1874 to oversee elementary education erected the Marmion Schools in Marmion Street and converted the Wesleyan Chapel in Bolebridge Street. In 1879 a School of Industry was founded in Marmion Street chiefly using money raised from a bazaar organised by Lady Emily Peel and other ladies prominent in Tamworth society. Further boys schools opened in Bolehall in 1891 and Hospital Street in 1897. Schools were subject to increasing standardisation and centralised control. An Act of 1902 transferred Tamworth's School Board responsibilities to Staffordshire County Council.

Increased educational opportunities led to a rise in literacy levels. A group of Tamworth ladies formed their own Book Society. Rawlett's library transferred from its home in Guy's almshouses to the new Queen Elizabeth Grammar School in 1868. The *Tamworth Herald*, first published in 1868, was one of a number of local newspapers available in the Victorian town. In 1804 the 'Permanent Library' was established in George Street; members paid a joining fee and an annual subscription of one guinea, equivalent to renting a pew in St Editha's. In 1841, Sir Robert Peel (2nd Baronet) founded a library in Colehill which was open to men and women over the age of 14 years for a small quarterly fee paid in advance. Peel's library had a comfortable reading room where newspapers were available and a fire burned in the hearth on cold winter days. A series of evening readings organised by the library in the Town Hall attracted large audiences.

The Peel Library closed in 1874 suffering from a funding crisis. Sir Robert Peel (3rd Baronet), heavily in debt, unable to satisfy

110 *Thomas Cooke (1821-1905), the last tenant of Tamworth Castle. He relinquished his lease to enable the public purchase of the castle to go ahead.*

the Charity Commissioners about discrepancies in the Peel School Charity fund of which he was the sole trustee, and having recently lost his parliamentary seat, was not in a position to help. However, the collection of books was kept intact and formed the basis of a free public library service which began in 1882.

Castle Ownership

Robert Peel's industrial use of the castle at the beginning of the 1790s ruined the stone flagged floor of the Banqueting Hall but otherwise caused little permanent damage. A red-brick floor replaced the cracked flags, then softwood boards were laid, and in recent times a high quality hardwood floor has been substituted. A large-scale 16th-century mural on the north wall of the Great Hall was whitewashed over in 1783 and destroyed. The scene from the Arthurian romances showed Lancelot du Lac and Tarquin, a renegade knight, in combat on the meadow below the castle. More general decay was the result of neglect by a succession of absentee owners.

Previous Shirley, Compton and Townshend owners all had property elsewhere in the country and chose not to live at Tamworth. But George Townshend, the 2nd Marquis son of Lady Charlotte Compton, was excited by the romance of the castle he inherited in 1807. He disposed of much of the Townshend property in Norfolk and set about comprehensive refurbishment. Old chimneys, with the exception of a Jacobean stack beside the Banqueting Hall, were removed and the building was re-roofed. The whole of the second storey was redesigned. Traditional features were incorporated including a Tudor-style long gallery reminiscent of an age when such rooms were used for indoor games and exercise. Fifty-five heraldic panels were added to form a frieze above the 17th-century pine wainscoting of the state withdrawing-room representing the arms of the Ferrers family through the ages. Three larger panels above the fireplace show the family connection to the royal house of Scotland. Gardens were planted and the battlemented gatehouse lodge built as a formal entrance from Holloway with a carriage house nearby. Work ceased when Townshend died in 1811. His heir, George, the 3rd Marquis had been disinherited after

111   *Opening of the castle, 1899. William Legge, Earl of Dartmouth and Lord Lieutenant of Staffordshire, officially declared Tamworth Castle open to the public on Whitsun Bank Holiday Monday, 22 May 1899. Lady Dartmouth is carrying the bouquet; on her right is Courtenay Warner MP with William MacGregor between; on her left Lord Dartmouth, Mrs Sculthorpe, Dr Sculthorpe and Philip Muntz MP.*

the breakdown of his marriage to Jane Dunn Gardiner. Within a year of the wedding, Lady Jane had run off to Gretna Green and contracted a second, bigamous marriage but she claimed the child born afterwards was conceived by George and took legal action to have her son recognised as Townshend's heir. The case dragged on until eventually the House of Lords rejected her claim. In the meantime, the castle remained empty until Chancery intervened and ordered its sale.

The next owner was John Robins, a London auctioneer who bought it as a home for his daughter and her husband Thomas Bramall. Robins and Bramall took a keen interest in civic affairs but little further work was done at the castle beyond that already completed by the 2nd Marquis Townshend. Robins presented the Corporation with a clock for the Town Hall. Bramall served as a churchwarden at St Editha's, as a magistrate, member of the new council and as mayor.

After Robins died in 1831, the castle again remained empty for a couple of years before it was bought back by the Townshend trustees acting on behalf of Lord Charles Townshend, a long serving Member of Parliament for Tamworth. It was rented to Miss Hester Wolferstan who continued the

Castle visitors book. The opening pages record the names of the dignitaries attending the grand opening ceremony.

repairs left unfinished in 1811. When Miss Wolferstan died in 1869 the castle was occupied briefly by Mr E. Wood before the last tenant moved in with his family, local businessman Thomas Cooke.

Cooke had renewed his lease in 1890 so it had another 14 years to run, but when the corporation began negotiating with the Townshend estate to purchase the castle for the town as a way of marking Queen Victoria's Diamond Jubilee he agreed to give up his home. Legal action against John Townshend (5th Marquis) appears to have forced a transfer of ownership before an agreement could be reached but as a result of the case the castle was put up for sale by auction. Other interested buyers were discouraged from bidding by a local crowd eager to see the castle in public hands and it was knocked down to the corporation at a price of just £3,000. On Whitsun Bank Holiday Monday 1899, amid a fanfare of publicity, the castle was officially declared open to the public by William Legge, Earl of Dartmouth and Lord Lieutenant of Staffordshire.

Nine

WAR AND PEACE: AUSTERITY AND THE LAST SIR ROBERT PEEL

As the 20th century dawned progress was apparent. Tamworth was a lively self-sufficient town of just over seven thousand inhabitants, with trades and businesses of all descriptions flourishing in the local area. The recently formed Co-operative Society had outgrown its humble beginnings and moved to sparkling new premises on the corner of Church Street and Colehill, its façade proudly sporting Gibbs and Canning decorative architectural stoneware and its entrance awash with Minton tiles.

Most tradespeople used horses and carts to transport a variety of goods direct to customers' doors. Freshly baked bread was delivered along with the occasional bucket of organic 'by product' for the garden. But horse power was being replaced: regular rail

113 *Co-operative Society delivery van. Motor vehicles began to take over from horses as the 20th century progressed.*

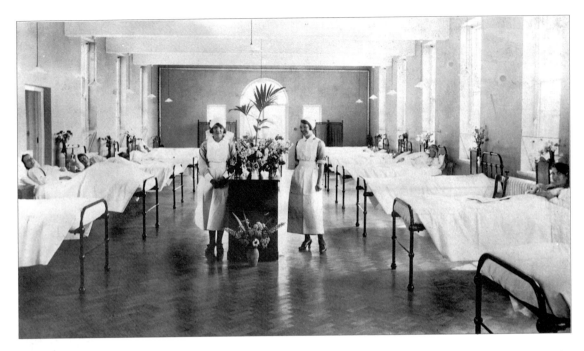

114   *General Hospital, Women's Ward 1923. Local subscriptions helped develop the Cottage Hospital into Tamworth General with its own operating theatre.*

115   *The Theatre, corner of Church Street and Lower Gungate. Built in 1798, it became a Baptist chapel and a malthouse before temporarily reverting to an entertainment venue as Tamworth Arts Centre from 1975 to 2001.*

services ran to all the major cities; motor cars appeared on the roads; passengers boarded the first motor omnibus; aircraft were spotted in the skies overhead. Pavements were flagged and streets were lit at night. St Editha's church and the castle had gas lighting installed. Public health benefited from a fresh water supply and underground drainage. By 1908 a sewage treatment plant in Coton was operational. Beneath the Town Hall, the former cell was converted into a public toilet. An operating theatre was added to an enlarged Cottage Hospital, which became the 'General'. Patients requiring treatment no longer faced the rigours of a trip to Birmingham. Borough Council involvement in housing began with a small development of 12 properties in what became Bradford Street.

A barn in Lichfield Street and occasionally the Town Hall had served as makeshift theatres. From 1798 until 1870 'The Theatre' on the corner of Church Street and Lower Gungate hosted productions. Some performances attracted the stars of the day such as Sarah Siddons and Harriet Mellon. Others featured less well-known players recreating big-name performances from the recent past, such as 'Mr Kemble's *Hamlet*' (Roger Kemble, manager of a famous troupe of actors was the father of Sarah Siddons). Almost two decades after the closure of the Theatre as a venue the Assembly Rooms opened on Corporation Street. Building had been prompted by Queen Victoria's Golden Jubilee. William Tait, landlord of the *Coffee Pot Inn*, George Street, launched a Palace of Varieties. From 1910, a mixture of live music hall variety shows and the latest silent movies, or 'flickers', were on offer at the Palace 'electric' Cinema in George Street.

In 1905, the free library moved to new premises paid for by American philanthropist, Andrew Carnegie. A horticultural society attracted a crowd of around three thousand to its annual show. Tamworth Cricket Club, founded in the 1850s just after over-arm bowling was adopted, was enjoying success. Branches of the Young Men's Christian Association and Young Women's Christian Association were open to young townspeople from 1872. Tamworth Castle Bowling Club played on a secluded green off Lady Bank, and from 1900 players were within earshot of the newly erected bandstand in the Castle Pleasure Grounds.

A High School for Girls was set up in 1910 on the College Lane site of the former National School, but within three years the

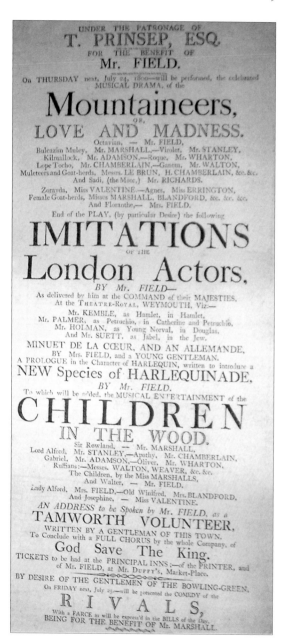

116 *Theatre notice, 1800. Regular productions featuring well-known actors attracted full houses to the newly opened playhouse.*

school had moved to new premises off Salters Lane. Meanwhile the grammar school had run into financial difficulties and control was transferred to the County Council.

Plans to mark the millennium of the fortification of Tamworth by Aethelfleda, believed by many to be the anniversary of the founding of the castle, were made in 1913. The Council appointed a committee to oversee arrangements and launched an appeal for public subscriptions; more than £300 was raised. Part of the fund was allocated to cover the cost of a memorial monument, a statue of Aethelfleda and the boy Athelstan by sculptor Edward George Bramwell, a former Tamworth art student, to a design by local stonemason Henry Charles Mitchell. Earl Ferrers performed the unveiling ceremony in the Castle Grounds on 9 July, officially launching a two-day millennary pageant. But events in Europe were about to intrude on the domestic agenda.

117 *Bandstand, Castle Pleasure Grounds. A bandstand overlooking the river was added in 1900.*

THE CALL OF THE NAVY!

1.

There is no need to implore a man to save his mother and sisters from murder and outrage. **He does not say he can't bother about them.** No! He goes off at full speed to their rescue.

If Germany win (and no game is won until it IS won) Germany would treat your mother and sisters worse than she treated Belgium. Germany says so.

2.

There is no need to implore a man to accept a good job. He does not reply that he has no use for money. No! He goes off to secure his chance.

If Germany win she will take care to get our trade and our Colonies, **for Germany started war mainly as a thieving expedition,** and your Unions would have no trade left and no money to fight for.

3.

There is no need to implore a man to rescue his mates from a burning mine. He does not reply that **they must look after themselves.** No! He rushes to their rescue in true English fashion.

If Germany win she would have gas-poisoned or bayoneted your mates left alone to struggle without reinforcements.

In a word, a man will risk anything for his mother, for money, and for his mates.

Now, note we are imploring you on their behalf to enlist.

Englishmen's duty to-day is to obey (**it is even the duty of Newspaper Editors**) and keep united.

Kitchener says "Enlist"!!! Therefore enlist!!!

One should be too proud to let another man's sons do one's share.

Your son may have to say sadly in years to come "My Father did not fight in the Great War. I can't understand why."

Turn up at 33 Bolebridge Street.

FELIX HAMEL, R.N.V.R.,
Hon. Recruiter.

"GOD SAVE THE KING."

Tamworth Herald Co. Ltd., 14 Silver Street, Tamworth.

ST. JOHN'S,

TAMWORTH,

September, 1914.

Dear

May I enlist your sympathy and generosity on behalf of the poor Belgian Refugees who have been driven to seek hospitality in England, owing to the terrible state of desolation to which their own country has been reduced.

Acting through the Birmingham Branch of the War Refugee Committee, I have volunteered to find a home and maintenance for a certain number of families until such time as they are enabled to return to their own country, These poor creatures have seen their homes and their possessions ruthlessly destroyed—they have experienced terrible sufferings and privations, and they are now entirely dependent on our hospitality; their one comfort is that the members of a family have so far been able to cling to one another, and this consolation we cannot take from them; consequently I am anxious to rent a large house in which four or five families may live together and be supported as long as is needful.

A small Committee has been formed to care for their welfare, upon which the Mayoress of Tamworth has graciously consented to act. The members of the Committee are:—Mrs. Allton, Mrs. Mundy, Mrs. Woodcock, Miss Bratt, Miss Emery, Miss Edith Emery, and Miss Graham Trotter.

Will you be so kind as to send me a donation for this object, or better still, to promise a certain sum weekly as long as it may be needed.

If you will send me a postcard I will arrange for a collector to call on you weekly or monthly for your offering.

I am, dear

Yours faithfully,

HENRY D. YEO.

118 *Recruiting poster, 1914. Almost one in four eligible men had volunteered to join the armed forces by the time conscription was introduced in 1916.*

119 *Appeal on behalf of Belgian refugees. The Reverend Henry Yeo, priest at St John's church, led the public appeal for help with housing and feeding families of Belgian refugees fleeing mainland Europe.*

The First World War

On 4 August 1914 Germany invaded Belgium and the Great War began. Three days later Lord Kitchener, newly appointed Secretary for War, made an impassioned plea for volunteers to join the armed forces. Local appeals followed. Felix Hamel became an honorary recruiting officer for the Naval Reserve. Almost one in four of all local men aged between 15 and 49 years had enlisted by the time conscription was introduced in 1916, a patriotic gesture on a grand scale. With pay in the services poor by comparison with what could be earned in civilian employment – a miner's wage, for example, averaged four or five times that of an army private or a naval rating – it was definitely duty calling and not the money.

In September the first refugees from mainland Europe, two Belgian families, arrived in Tamworth. A call for help led by the Reverend Henry Yeo, priest of St John's church, met with a generous response. The Co-operative Society placed a house at number 8 Colehill at the disposal of one family and Mr E. Morgan of the *Castle Hotel* offered a cottage on Gungate for use by the other.

Plans for a new theatre with an auditorium capable of seating 700, already in hand when war was declared, went ahead and the Grand opened with a charity concert in aid of Serbian sick and wounded in 1915. The building had terracotta facings by Gibbs and Canning and was topped by a statue of a Greek goddess, upraised arms holding a gas-fed lamp aloft. Because of the danger posed by Zeppelin raids the lamp could not be lit, but otherwise the theatre operated as intended, mainly as a cinema.

Six hundred and ninety-three local men gave their lives in the conflict. Many more were wounded and a regular flow of casualties sent home for treatment stretched the

120 & 121   *The Grand Theatre, George Street opened on Wednesday 19 May 1915 with a concert in aid of Serbian sick and wounded. The building had Gibbs and Canning terracotta facings and was topped by the statue of a Greek goddess. Inside there was plush tip-up seating for 700; and the Reverend Maurice Peel memorial window, St Editha's church. The town vicar won two Military Crosses during the First World War but lost his life to a sniper's bullet in 1917. This memorial window in the north aisle of St Editha's was designed by Henry Holiday of the Arts and Crafts movement and made at their Whitefriars Studio by James Powell and Son.*

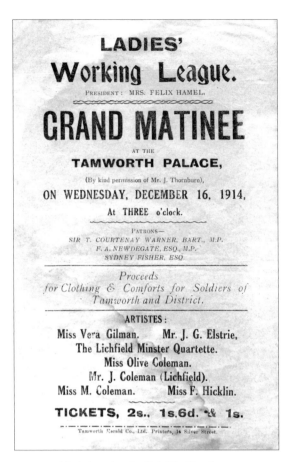

LADIES' Working League.

PRESIDENT: MRS. FELIX HAMEL.

GRAND MATINEE

AT THE

TAMWORTH PALACE,

(By kind permission of Mr. J. Thornburn),

ON WEDNESDAY, DECEMBER 16, 1914,

At THREE o'clock.

PATRONS—
SIR T. COURTENAY WARNER, BART., M.P.
F. A. NEWDEGATE, ESQ., M.P.
SYDNEY FISHER, ESQ.

Proceeds
for Clothing & Comforts for Soldiers of
Tamworth and District.

ARTISTES:

Miss Vera Gilman.   Mr. J. G. Elstrie,
The Lichfield Minster Quartette.
Miss Olive Coleman.
Mr. J. Coleman (Lichfield).
Miss M. Coleman.   Miss F. Hicklin.

TICKETS, 2s., 1s. 6d. & 1s.

Tamworth Herald Co., Ltd. Printers, 14 Silver Street.

BOROUGH OF TAMWORTH.

Maximum Retail Prices of Home-killed Meat, prescribed by the Food Control Committee, from November 1st, 1917.

BEEF.	per lb.	VEAL.	per lb.
Sirloin	1/6	Legs - - -	1/4
Round, whole joints -	1/6	Fillet - - -	1/8
Rump - -	1/6	Loins - - -	1/6
„ (undercut or aitch bone)	1/5	Shoulder - -	1/1
„ Steak (without bone)	1/9	Neck, whole - -	1/3
Round Steak (without bone)	1/7	„ best end -	1/6
„ „ (with bone)	1/6	„ thin end -	-/10
Blade bone Steak (without bone)	1/5	Breast - -	1/-
Thick Flank - -	1/5	Knuckle - -	-/8
„ „ (front side)	1/6	Liver - -	1/3
„ „ (rear side)	1/4	**MUTTON AND LAMB.**	
Thin Flank - -	1/1	Legs - - -	1/6
Ribs - -	1/6	Shoulder - -	1/4
„ (flat) - -	1/1	Half shoulder (straight side)	1/5
Cross cut, top ribs -	1/4	„ „ (round side)	1/4
Brisket - -	1/1	Loins - -	1/6
Neck, boiling (with bone) -	-/11	Neck, whole - -	1/3
Gravy Beef (with bone) -	-/8	„ best end -	1/6
„ „ (without bone) -	1/2	„ middle -	1/4
Clod of Beef, blade -	1/2	„ thin end -	1/-
Shoulder or Crop -	1/4	Breast, whole -	-/10
Kidney Suet - -	1/2	„ chops -	1/-
Caul „ -	-/11	Loin chops -	1/8
Liver - -	1/-	Liver - -	1/2
Kidney - -	1/6		

The above prices are for the first grade quality and for cash only.
Any infringement of the above Order should be reported to the undersigned.

JOHN MATTHEWS,
Executive Officer.

Borough Food Office,
21, Church Street, Tamworth,
25th October, 1917.

122 *Matinée notice, Ladies' Working League, 1914. Members of the Women's Liberal Association formed Tamworth Ladies' Working League. Concerts were organised to raise funds and provide 'comforts for our soldiers and sailors'.*

123 *Meat prices, 1917. Meat prices were capped to prevent profiteering in the closing months of the First World War as a spate of panic-buying led to shortages. Limits were imposed on the amount of tea, butter and sugar that could be bought.*

facilities of Tamworth General Hospital. One of those who paid the ultimate price was the Reverend Maurice Peel, killed in 1917 attempting to help wounded soldiers on a muddy, blood-soaked battlefield in northern France. The Reverend Peel, cousin of the 4th Baronet, was a widower with two small children, Mary and David. Wounded at the Battle of Festubert in the Ypres Salient, he returned home in 1915 to become the vicar of St Editha's. Peel went back to the Western Front, in January 1917 aged 43, with the 1st Royal Fusiliers. Accompanying his battalion into action carrying nothing but his walking stick, he won two Military Crosses for his bravery. In May of that year a sniper's bullet struck as he went about his task in no-man's land. It was two days before his body was recovered and buried after a brief battlefield ceremony.

At home, local volunteers set up a reserve force. Members of the Women's Liberal

Association formed the Tamworth Ladies' Working League to provide 'comforts for our soldiers and sailors'. Raising funds from concerts held at the Grand Theatre and Palace Cinema, the league supplied clothes and also carried out hospital visits. With so many men away on active service, gender barriers in employment began to break down. Women took over jobs, for example as bus conductors, previously considered 'men's work'.

German U-boat activity disrupted food imports but a bumper harvest in 1917 and a general increase in home-produced food maintained supplies. Potatoes and sugar became scarce but rationing could probably have been avoided if a spate of panic-buying had not led to shortages at the beginning of 1918. As a result sales of tea, butter and margarine were subject to limits during the final months of hostilities to conserve stocks. Meat prices were capped to prevent profiteering.

Peace was concluded on 11 November 1918 but it was a while before normality returned. The Armistice was officially celebrated in the Castle Pleasure Grounds the following summer with a full day's programme of music and events.

The End of Drayton Manor and the Last of the Peels

By the 1900s Drayton Manor was little more than an empty shell, only a handful of the 78 rooms now furnished. Cost-cutting measures were in place and most of the 'family silver' and much of the land had been sold. A small army of servants and estate staff had been reduced to around a dozen. To raise cash the grounds were opened to a paying public. One

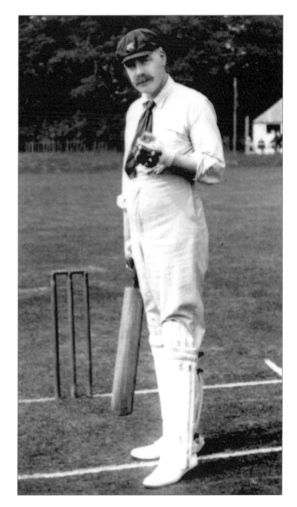

124   *Sir Robert Peel, 4th Baronet (1867-1925), opening the innings at the Deer Park Ground, Drayton Manor in the 1920s.*

event featured daredevil Dolly Shephard, who thrilled an enormous crowd by ascending in a hot-air balloon before parachuting back to earth.

Sir Robert Peel (4th Baronet) had fallen out with the rector of St Peter's church at Drayton Bassett, and the wedding of his son and heir to Canadian actress Beatrice Lillie, 'the funniest woman in the world' according to Noel Coward, took place at St Paul's church, Fazeley in 1920. John and Lucie Lillie came over from Toronto to see their daughter married but Sir Robert, by now in poor health, did not attend the service. He died in 1925. Robert junior had resigned his commission in the Coldstream Guards in 1918, but preferred the family flat in London to Drayton Manor. His serious financial situation left little room for manoeuvre. The ancestral home was sold and all the buildings were demolished apart from the clock tower, that had been not only an architectural feature but also a practical way of letting workmen know when to start and stop work in the days when large numbers were employed on the estate.

Peel earned a living touring the country with his Harmony Dance Band featuring the vocal talents of the 'Bing Boys' until his death in 1935. Beatrice Lillie brought flowers to his grave at Drayton Bassett twice a year into her own old age. Their son was destined to be the sixth and last Sir Robert Peel by direct descent. He was killed on active service with HMS *Tenedos* in 1942. The ship was anchored in Colombo Harbour, Ceylon [Sri Lanka] when it came under aerial bombardment from the Japanese. Peel's body was never found and for long afterwards his mother refused to give up hope that he might miraculously return.

The General Strike

Unemployment rocketed in the economic 'slump' of the 1920s. For those lucky enough to have work, wages were often low. In 1925, colliery owners announced their intention to slash coalminers' wages. Stanley Baldwin, the Prime Minister, urged restraint and set up a Royal Commission to investigate the industry's problems. In the meantime pay was subsidised from the public purse. When the Commission concluded that miners' wages

should be reduced, the scene was set for conflict. In April 1926 mine owners drew up new conditions of employment based on longer hours for less pay. It was a 'take it or leave it' deal: accept the new terms by 1 May or the pit gates would be locked. The Trades Union Congress responded by calling a General Strike of workers in key industries in support of the miners from 3 May. A Tamworth Strike Committee was formed. Public transport came to a standstill and the workforce at Fisher's paper mills downed

125 *Sir Robert Peel, 5th Baronet (1898-1934) and Beatrice Lillie (1894-1989), pictured at Drayton Manor with their pet Alsatian dog. Peel and the Canadian-born actress were married at St Paul's church, Fazeley in 1920.*

tools. For ten days there was stalemate, but faced with a tough stance from the government the TUC backed down, urging settlement and a return to work.

The General Strike was over, leaving the miners to continue the dispute alone. Mass meetings were held in the Castle Pleasure Grounds. Arthur Cook, general secretary of the Miners Federation and a firebrand speaker, was cheered when he came personally to address one of the gatherings.

Miners received a small weekly allowance from their union but it was not enough. Hardship set in as the weeks passed. The Board of Guardians in charge of poor relief agreed to payments for wives and children. Workers at Tamworth Co-operative Society contributed to a fund to provide food vouchers. Soup kitchens opened in the Assembly Rooms and in chapels. Both the Working Men's Club and Progressive Club provided meals to members in need.

Feelings naturally ran high. As men began to straggle back to work, cases of intimidation came before the courts. On one occasion the Riot Act was read before an angry group of miners gathered outside the gates of Pooley Hall Colliery. Women too were passionate about the cause. A group of miners' wives appeared before magistrates charged with threatening to throw a strikebreaker into the canal.

By the beginning of June, over half the workforce of around seven hundred miners at the largest local colliery, Pooley Hall, had abandoned the strike and returned. A work train known as the 'Paddy' once more ran a regular service from the town's railway station to Kingsbury Colliery. Beauchamp, Amington, Tame Valley, Birch Coppice and

Alvecote were all winding coal. The strike was crumbling but it was the end of November before the last few strikers admitted defeat and accepted revised pay and conditions. Many of those who held out until the end faced victimisation. A few never worked in the pits again.

Between the Wars

In 1920, the old Castle Mill complex was demolished and a flower garden, tennis courts and putting green were built on the site. A decade later the Castle Pleasure Grounds were opened extending south of the river on a reclaimed stretch of boggy flood plain formerly used as a rubbish tip.

While the miners strike was in progress, Pooley Hall Colliery turned its thoughts to diversifying and to maintaining a reputation for work of public benefit. Electricity was proving popular in towns elsewhere and a limited supply was already available locally. The Polesworth Colliery muscled in on the Leicestershire and Warwickshire Electric Power Company, the authorised suppliers locally, and offered to extend a mains supply throughout the borough. Tamworth Gaslight and Coke Company mounted a vigorous campaign against the idea, claiming gas was cheaper and safer, but the Council seized the opportunity. By the mid-1930s electricity had replaced gas lighting in the streets, the first traffic lights in town were controlling vehicles at the crossroads where Aldergate, Church Street, Lichfield Street and Silver Street meet, and Tamworth and District Electric Supply Company (TADESCO) was open for business in Church Street.

Tamworth's position at the confluence of two rivers always made it vulnerable to

126 *Carnival float, 1933. Local businesses including Gibbs and Canning decorated lorries and used the carnival to advertise their products.*

flooding in severe weather. Major floods occurred in 1878, 1900, 1912 and 1928. The worst of recent times took place in May 1932. A 24-hour downpour left low-lying areas cut off. Parts of Bolebridge Street were under a metre of water.

Borough boundaries were extended again in 1932. A shortage of houses, slum clearance and the availability of government subsidies spurred large-scale council housing projects. Between the wars around eight hundred new

homes were built. In 1936, a further girls senior school was built at Perrycrofts. As development continued famous landmarks began to disappear. Victorian Bole Bridge was replaced and one of the oldest and best-known buildings in the town centre, the Paregoric Shop, a 14th-century timber-framed house in Church Street, was demolished. Paregoric was a popular medicine in the 1920s and '30s. Made chiefly from opium and camphor and flavoured with aniseed, it was supplied as a drink or mixed with gum in a lozenge and used to treat upset stomachs. The Paregoric Shop had an oversailing jetty, a practical solution to the problem of building upper storeys in early medieval times. Because joists were laid flat, like planking, they were very springy; creating an overhang by projecting the joists beyond the edge of the building reduced the bounce and provided extra interior space. It was not until Jacobean times that the jetty was replaced as a design feature and the stability achieved by laying joists with the narrow side down was exploited.

In 1933 Tamworth Football Club was formed, and an open-air swimming pool opened in the Castle Pleasure Grounds in 1937. Local pit workers paid their own tribute to the nursing care at Tamworth General Hospital by contributing funds to have a nurses' home built on site. Rawlett's 17th-century library, by now of antiquarian interest rather than educational value, was auctioned by the trustees and the money raised added to the charity's funds.

With a dream and a garden shed for a workshop, Thomas Williams, a talented engineer and designer formerly with the Raleigh Cycle Company, began what was to become the Reliant Motor Company. Raleigh had dropped their plans to develop three-wheeled vehicles but Williams was convinced they were wrong and that a market existed for the right product. His prototype three-wheeled van was licensed on 1 January 1935. Within four years the company had moved to a plant at Two Gates on the former Midland Red bus garage site and was building its own side-valve 747cc engines. Production was halted from 1939-

45 when the Ministry of Defence called upon Reliant's expertise and the factory switched to machining parts in support of the war effort.

Reliant Engineering was not the first vehicle manufacturer in the area: Johnson Brothers, who began making bicycles in College Lane, switched to motor cars and produced vehicles into the 1930s from a garage workshop at 7 Aldergate.

As an antidote to the persistent problems of short-time working and high unemployment endemic throughout the previous decade, a carnival was organised in 1931. Ten days of special events and competitions culminated in a day of festivities in the Castle Pleasure Grounds. Carnival day began with a procession of floats entered by local businesses vying for the honour of being judged the best decorated. The carnival proved so popular it became an annual summer fixture until the storm clouds of war necessitated cancellation of the 1939 event. Renee Dodd, already chosen as Carnival Queen for that year, never got to wear her crown.

The Second World War
Although there was mounting tension in Europe during the 1930s, to most people war seemed unthinkable. In 1937, Boy Scouts from Tamworth visited Germany and hosted a return trip by members of the Hitler Youth. Nevertheless, some preparations were made. An Air Raid Precautions service (ARP) was formed. When war did break out in 1939 everyone was issued with an identity card and a gas mask. Aerial attack was the initial fear and the ARP was quickly mobilised. Nightly 'blackouts' were enforced; windows

127   *Pillbox, Lady Meadow. This hexagonal design (Type FW3/24) could house seven armed men. Thick walls of reinforced concrete were capable of withstanding tank and artillery shells. It was built to guard Lady Bridge and the river crossing in the event of an invasion believed imminent in the dark days of 1940, and was regularly manned by Home Guard volunteers.*

were covered with black paper or a blackout curtain in order to avoid any chance of attracting enemy aircraft. Street lamps were turned off and vehicle headlamps masked. Bombs caused damage close to Fazeley Road and in Manor Road, Bolehall. Alders Mill and the railway station both suffered near misses.

Merchant shipping came under fierce attack leading to food shortages and widespread rationing was introduced from January 1940 to prevent uncertainty and ensure equal treatment. Restrictions on the amounts of bacon, butter and sugar that could be bought were soon followed by limits on meat, fish, tea, jam, biscuits, cereals, eggs, milk, cheese, tinned fruit, chocolate and sweets. Children were allowed extra milk and orange juice. Everyone was issued with a ration book. Despite the constraints, what was available made up a wholesome, balanced diet and the overall health of the nation improved as a result.

The government's 'Dig for Victory' campaign encouraged people to cultivate their gardens, dig up lawns and flowerbeds and keep chickens, rabbits and other livestock. Faced with a shortage of farm labour, it established the Women's Land Army. Various women's groups undertook charitable work, knitting clothes and helping salvage metal, paper, rags and other items that might be usefully recycled to help the war effort.

Spring 1940 was arguably our darkest hour. The German army had met little resistance in France, Belgium and the Netherlands and was now poised across the English Channel. Invasion was a real threat and plans to counter an assault were prepared as a matter of urgency.

Over two hundred men not eligible for active service in the regular forces enrolled at the Police Station in Church Street to form a Local Defence Volunteer force, later to become the Home Guard. National defences concentrated on protecting the coastline and London. Just one thin 'stop line' was planned in the Midlands, a last ditch defensive line across southern Staffordshire protecting the strategic road and rail routes northwards.

Local contractors with help from the Royal Engineers hurriedly constructed reinforced concrete pillboxes to guard river crossings on the Tame and eastwards along the River Trent. There are several different pillbox designs. Those built in this area, including the box on Lady Meadow protecting Lady Bridge, are a hexagonal type, design code FW3/24. Loopholes on each side provide all-round vision for men armed with light machine guns and rifles. But, until First World War weaponry and munitions from the United States became available, most volunteers had only makeshift weapons.

An air-raid siren installed in the tower of the electric showrooms regularly sent people scurrying for cover as the Luftwaffe ran bombing sorties. Trench shelters were constructed in Bolehall Park and the Castle Pleasure Grounds. A new fire station was built on the corner of Lichfield Street and Wardle Street. The local brigade became part of a National Fire Service for the duration of the war, transferring to Staffordshire County Council control afterwards. Beneath the Town Hall the old butter market area where the fire engine had previously been kept was opened up and the arches filled with sandbags to provide a temporary shelter in the centre of town during air raids.

Over two and a half thousand children, evacuated mainly from the West Midlands, north-west England and the south-eastern corner of the country, were billeted with local families. Half-cylindrical, corrugated-iron Nissen huts at Two Gates housed prisoners-of-war. The camp was later converted into a hostel for displaced people, many of them eastern Europeans unwilling or unable to return to Soviet-occupied countries. Officially classified as emergency workers rather than refugees, they were recruited from camps in Germany to help meet labour shortages in industry. Those arriving at Two Gates were trained as colliery workers.

128 *Prisoner-of-war camp, Two Gates. Nissen huts of corrugated iron housed prisoners during the Second World War. The camp was converted after the war into a hostel for displaced people recruited as colliery workers. The smaller hut in the centre of this picture was the toilet block.*

By the time the war was over, 340 local men had died. Victory in Europe was hastened immeasurably by the cracking of the Enigma code. Colin Grazier, an Able Seaman from Two Gates, was among the crew aboard HMS *Petard* pursuing a German U-boat. They caught up with the vessel in the eastern Mediterranean. Badly damaged, the submarine was forced to surface. As its crew abandoned ship, Colin Grazier and two colleagues swam to the vessel and began searching below decks. Battling against time as the stricken submarine took on water, they managed to recover the vital codebooks and pass them out before U559 was swamped, with Colin Grazier and Lieutenant Tony

Fasson still aboard. Their heroism undoubtedly saved many lives and helped to shorten the war. Even in death they 'did their bit', posthumously being granted the George Cross instead of the Victoria Cross that their action deserved to avoid alerting the enemy to the real significance of what they had achieved.

Victory was celebrated with street parties, decorations, concerts and an agricultural show. Illuminations were particularly welcome after years of blackout and the castle was floodlit. Food supplies slowly returned to normal but some rationing continued until 1954. It was 1951, the year of the Festival of Britain, before a carnival was held again.

The Post-War Era

More housing projects began with an estate on Amington Road. Education facilities continued to increase. In 1956, the Further Education College in Upper Gungate opened. Four years later the grammar school and girls high school merged and there was a new secondary school for boys on Ashby Road. Former school buildings beside the entrance to the parish church were demolished to open up St Editha's Close.

With increasing urbanisation, business at the livestock smithfield in Victoria Road declined and the cattle market closed. Industry continued to develop locally. A transmitter at Sutton Coldfield beamed the first television signals to the town. Vans began to roll off the production line at Reliant once more, followed by the first passenger cars. Aluminium, fibreglass and pressure-moulded plastic bodies were introduced into the innovative Reliant range.

Gibbs and Canning's scantily clad terracotta goddess came down from her perch on the Grand when the theatre closed and the building was pulled down in 1958.

Social policy was changed forever by the 1948 National Assistance Act. Poor relief and the threat of the workhouse were finally abolished. Hospital services were taken over by the new National Health Service. Concerned about unchecked urban sprawl around the big cities, the government passed

129 *Gibbs and Canning statue. The scantily clad Venus was rescued by demolition men from her perch above the Grand when the theatre was pulled down in 1958 and is now on show as part of the Tamworth Story Exhibition at the castle.*

a series of planning acts between 1947 and 1952. It led to an overspill agreement between Tamworth and local authorities in Birmingham and the West Midlands that was to change the face of the town.

Ten

Overspill, Expansion and Tamworth Today

During the Second World War the government assumed sweeping powers. Almost every aspect of life was directed, from the food people ate and the clothes they wore, to the jobs people did and the way they were entertained. In many ways the Town and Country Planning regulations that followed in the immediate post-war period were a continuation of this centralised control. Yet to those involved it did not feel like being part of some social engineering scheme. The first 'overspill' tenants – nicknamed the '021s' – arrived in 1959, mostly 20-something couples attracted by affordable housing and the prospect of a better quality of life.

The earliest apartment blocks were grim, soulless concrete mistakes that were soon replaced. In contrast, the multi-storey riverside flats off Lichfield Street built in 1967-8, though characterised as 'tower blocks' and unpopular with some for their intrusion on the skyline, are thoughtfully designed and among the best of their type. A thousand houses were springing up each year during the early 1970s. Borough boundaries were extended yet again to embrace more of the surrounding villages and in 1974 a new Borough Charter created the Tamworth District of Staffordshire. Burlington House was acquired as the new Borough Council's administrative centre and renamed Marmion House.

Much of Tamworth's historic centre was bulldozed. Ancient buildings in Gungate, Market Street, Church Street, George Street, Silver Street and Bolebridge Street were cleared to make way for pedestrian precincts, shopping centres and retail arcades. Mrs Hutton's fountain, long redundant as a drinking trough but still a popular meeting place, was an early victim of road widening and traffic management schemes.

In 1960, the Borough Council in partnership with river authorities implemented a major flood prevention scheme. New floodbanks were built alongside the rivers and flood relief channels cut. The severest test came in November 2000. Torrential rain caused widespread disruption on road and rail. Water levels rose alarmingly. The Tame and Anker both burst their banks. Car parks at Lady Bridge and Leisure Island were inundated but the flood defences largely contained the floodwater and successfully protected residential and industrial areas.

Schools had to keep pace with a population calculated to grow from forty thousand in 1971 to approaching eighty thousand three decades later. In 1978, the grammar, Perrycrofts, and Mercian schools came together to form a single comprehensive secondary unit. Rawlett School opened in 1981.

Tamworth's grand Victorian railway station was replaced by a rather less imposing but functional concrete building. Magistrates heard their last case in the upper room of the old Town Hall and in 1970 moved to purpose-built courts in Spinning School Lane. Five years later new police headquarters opened next door. At the beginning of the 1980s the carnival had ceased to be a big attraction and looked set to fade away until the Lions Club stepped in to breathe new life into proceedings.

Out-of-town superstores arrived in the late 1980s when Ventura Park was developed at Bitterscote. A Health Centre was built on Upper Gungate in 1967. Sir Robert Peel District Hospital at Mile Oak opened in 1996 and within two years had taken over all local hospital services. The frontages of St Editha's on Comberford Road and the General on Hospital Street were preserved when the sites were redeveloped to provide housing.

The town's appliances were converted to North Sea gas. One by one, the giant gasometers dominating Bolebridge Street and Mill Lane were demolished. The last of the holders vanished in 1985 and Saxon Mill grew on the reclaimed 'brownfield' site.

In 1991, the ten-screen UCI complex opened in the Palace Media Centre, Bolebridge Street. When Tamworth Snow Dome and Peaks Leisure Centre opened in 1994 it offered customers the first indoor ski surface in Europe with real snow. The refurbished Territorial Army Drill Hall in Corporation Street, renamed in honour of Councillor Philip Dix OBE, former mayor

and leader of the Council, provides a focus for voluntary community services.

Reliant introduced the eccentric but much loved Robin and the quirky Bond Bug. In direct contrast to their range of lightweight economy vehicles, they also made the classic Scimitar, an icon of the fashion-conscious 1960s whose devotees famously included Princess Anne; over three hundred vehicles a week were rolling off the production line in the early 1980s. Then the company became caught up in a series of corporate takeovers that led to receivership despite full order books and a healthy turnover. Finally, in 1998, under new ownership and with a brand new range of vehicles planned, the company left its Tamworth base for a new factory at nearby Burntwood.

Famous names and in many cases whole industries vanished from the scene permanently. Gibbs and Canning closed their doors for the last time in the 1960s. The National Coal Board had wound down and shut most of the local collieries by 1965. Birch Coppice continued until 1987. Hamel's superfine tape and webbing mill remained a family business until the premises were sold in 1980; the mill was demolished the following year. Tolson's Mill was converted into an enterprise park housing a variety of small businesses in individual units. Four centuries of papermaking came to an end with the closure of Alders Mill in 1993.

New businesses were moving in to occupy the flexible units on newly constructed industrial estates, both large, established companies and also small enterprises, the lifeblood of the future economy. Tamworth had made a transition, from semi-rural town with plans for expansion to fully-fledged commercial and industrial centre.

Tamworth Today

Much of St Editha's church dates from the century of rebuilding after the fire of 1345, but succeeding ages have all left their mark, each generation adding a layer of history to this peaceful site of collective memory. The sculpted effigy of Dean Witney lies in St George's Chapel. In the recesses of the chancel lie stone representations of Joan Freville and of Baldwin Freville with his wife. Nearest the altar, Sir John and Lady Dorothy Ferrers recline in alabaster above a decorated tomb. All bear the scars of Puritan zeal. Ten statuettes remain of an original 12 in the canopied niches of the Ferrers' tomb. Each figure has been deliberately and systematically decapitated. A badly damaged freestone effigy in the north transept is believed to be a member of the Comberford family.

Just inside the west doorway, extensively remodelled around 1800, stands an extravagant memorial to Sir John Ferrers, who died in 1680, and his son Humphrey, drowned in the River Trent two years earlier. It is an exuberant, garlanded riot of polished marble complete with renaissance cherubs and heraldic arms. Lifesize statues of a man and woman, dressed in the senatorial togas of imperial Rome and wearing the flowing wigs in vogue in Restoration England, kneel either side of a Latin inscription composed by historian William Dugdale. The monument is the work of Grinling Gibbons and Arnold Quellin. Known primarily for his work in wood, Gibbons was master carver to the kings and queens of England. Patrons

130   *Ferrers memorial, St Editha's church. Just inside the west doorway of the parish church, this elaborate memorial to Sir John Ferrers and his son Humphrey is the work of master carver Grinling Gibbons.*

included Charles II, James II, William and Mary, Queen Anne and George I. The Ferrers memorial displays all the depth, sharpness and intricacy that made Gibbons, acknowledged as the best craftsman of his age, and arguably of any age, outstanding. The statues are by Caius Gabriel Cibber, equally famous in his day, whose representations of the Madnesses commissioned for the new Bedlam Hospital are now in the Victoria and Albert Museum. The memorial originally stood against the north wall of the chancel close to the altar. The lower portion of the

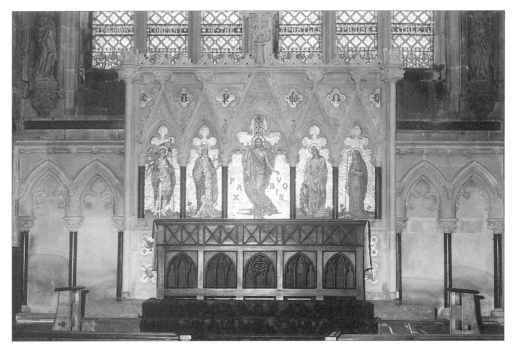

131 *Reredos, St Editha's church. Iridescent mosaic glass panels from the famous Venetian factory of Antonio Salviati form a striking backdrop to the altar in the parish church.*

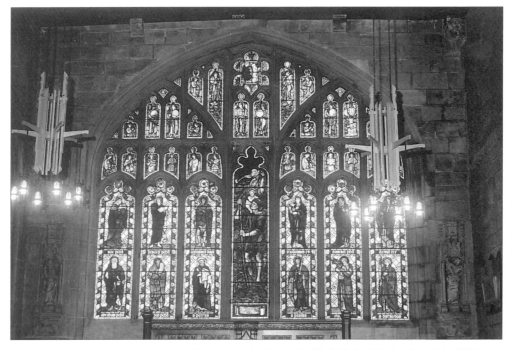

132 *Angels of Creation window, St Editha's church, designed by Ford Madox Ford and made by William Morris.*

west entrance supporting the tower contains older masonry from an earlier porch that has been deliberately chipped and scotched as if to provide a key for plaster, suggesting it may once have been painted.

The predominant architectural style of St Editha's is 'Decorated', characteristic of the 14th century when major construction work was carried out. Gothic tastes enjoyed a vogue in the 20th century and George Gilbert Scott was one of the architects inspired by Gothic revivalism. The font and the reredos or altar screen are to his designs. Statues carved by John Birnie Philip, sculptor of the Albert Memorial, flank a reredos of iridescent mosaic glass panels from the famous Venetian glass factory of Antonio Salviati.

The Arts and Crafts movement led by William Morris promoted handicrafts and functional art to the status of fine art. St Editha's contains excellent examples of all the leading craftsmen and artists linked to the movement. Three windows in the chancel clerestory describing the legend of St Editha in strikingly radiant stained glass were designed by Ford Madox Ford and made by William Morris. Morris also produced the 'Angels of Creation' window and the Reverend Brooke Lambert memorial window, both in St George's Chapel, to designs by Edward Burne-Jones. The north aisle has two memorial windows designed by Henry Holiday and made by James Powell and Son at their famous Whitefriars Studio in London. The latest addition to this superb collection of decorative glass is Alan Younger's west window above the entrance. This imaginative interpretation of 'the Holy City, the New Jerusalem', inspired by a passage in the book of *Revelation*, was unveiled by Princess Margaret in 1975.

An 18th-century restorer has left his own memorial 'W. Moggs 1752' on a beam high above the east window. Today's wooden roof is the result of restoration work carried out between 1990-2. Of four hundred original roof bosses, around a quarter were discovered to be missing; parishioners advertised for old oak pews and used the wood to hand carve replacements prior to gilding.

The 13th-century crypt of four vaulted bays supported by elegant chamfered ribs was converted from boiler room to coffee shop in 1977. A faded medieval inscription on the north wall written in Latin translates as 'O lord of wealth and power you will not live forever, do well while you live if you would live after death'. Beneath the verse an abbreviated form of '*Miserere* Jesus Christ' implores 'have mercy' in bold decorated letters. To which Marmion, Freville or Ferrers was this addressed?

Outside, high on the south wall, is a sundial, an 1822 replacement of an earlier model. By then, of course, the church had long since had its own clock, but dials, as well as being decorative, were still useful for resetting cumbersome mechanical timepieces in an age before the Greenwich 'pips'. At noon the gnomon, which is set at a precise angle equal to the co-latitude (the difference between the latitude of the church at 52° 38´ north and 90°), casts a vertical shadow downwards from the centre of the dial. Radiating lines mark the time in precisely calculated quarter-hour segments from 5.45a.m. to 5.15p.m. As you face the dial, morning hours are on the left of the central noon line, afternoon hours on the right.

133   *Inscription in the crypt, St Editha's church. The 13th-century crypt was incorporated in the main body of the church in the 15th century. A faded Latin inscription reminds an anonymous lord of his mortality and to live accordingly if he hopes for salvation. The large characters are an abbreviated form of the plea for mercy 'Miserere Jesus Christ'.*

134   *Sundial, St Editha's church. Mainly decorative but useful once for resetting cumbersome mechanical clocks and watches in the days before the Greenwich 'pips', this 1822 dial is calibrated to show the time from 5.45a.m. to 5.15p.m.*

Five bells housed in the tower at the time of the Reformation became six in the 17th century and seven in Victorian times. In 1932, all but one were removed for recasting and additions were made to create the ten-bell peal that can be heard ringing out across the town today. With a nod to Peel's landmark political version, a 'Spiritual Manifesto' in 1998 created a bond between denominations under the umbrella title of Tamworth Covenanting Churches.

Nothing now remains of the royal Saxon burh, but the Norman keep of the Marmions still presides over the town from its lofty perch. Fragments of the ruined deanery can be seen between brambles in the gardens that stretch from Lower Gungate towards the churchyard. A stretch of deanery wall continues alongside the Old Bell building, where a portion is exposed inside a shop, and peeps through onto Lower Gungate.

Almost hidden now between modern houses on Wigginton Road and Ashby Road is the tiny Spital Chapel, built by Philip Marmion in the 13th century. Or was an earlier building incorporated in Marmion's chantry? It is notoriously difficult to date masonry of the period. Shallow foundations

135 *Deanery wall, Lower Gungate. The end of one of the former deanery walls emerges at the side of the Old Bell building.*

136 *Spital Chapel, now almost hidden behind the modern houses of Wigginton Road and Ashby Road. An earlier Saxon or Norman building may lie at the core of Philip Marmion's 13th-century chantry foundation.*

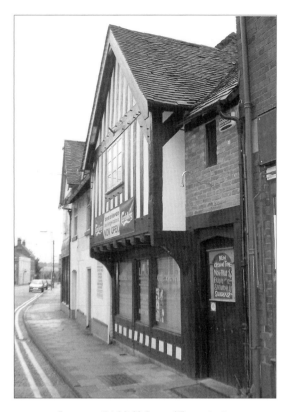

137 *Jetty, 111 Lichfield Street. The projecting upper-storey jetty of this 16th-century timber-framed building is a reminder of early construction techniques before joists were laid narrow side down.*

138 *Gazebo, the* Moat House. *This charming 18th-century building in the garden of the* Moat House *has a weathercock that connects to a compass chart painted on the ceiling.*

and nave walls three-quarters of a metre thick look Saxon. Other features, for example the north door rebate and the tooling of the stone in the chancel wall, suggest a 12th-century date. Spital Chapel is now linked to St Leonard's church, Wigginton and is used for Holy Communion services twice a month.

Beneath the Georgian *Old Stone Cross* public house, formerly the *Three Tuns* but near the site where the medieval market cross once stood, is a 16th-century groin-vaulted cellar of two bays that was once the undercroft of a high status Tudor house. The projecting upper-storey jetty of 111 Lichfield Street is a reminder of early building techniques and is

one of a number of well-preserved timber-framed 15th- and 16th-century houses in the town. Perhaps most prominent are those in Gungate and Little Church Lane. Others are hidden behind new frontages. Three capitals from Ionic pilasters and a stone fleur-de-lys carving from the Free Grammar School were saved when the school buildings were demolished and now adorn the brickwork of the shops built on the Lower Gungate site in 1970. The *Moat House*, converted into a restaurant, displays its impressive stepped gables behind an avenue of mature lime trees. No trace of the moat remains but the garden has an interesting 18th-century gazebo with a weathervane mounted on its pyramid-shaped roof that connects to a compass chart painted on the ceiling inside.

Tamworth's oldest nonconformist church, the Unitarian chapel in Victoria Road, is now shared with the local Royal Naval Association branch.

The old Town Hall is a prominent reminder of Thomas Guy's legacy, as are his almshouses, now extended and renovated but still occupying the corner of Spinning School Lane. In the upper room of the Town Hall, the former meeting room and council chamber houses a fine collection of portraits including Thomas Guy, Sir Robert Peel (2nd Baronet), Captain William Peel VC, John Peel MP, the Reverend John Rawlett, the Reverend Francis Blick and William Robinson. Robinson was a veterinary surgeon who worked for the royal household and was mayor of Tamworth on three occasions.

A repositioned milestone beside the wall surrounding the Health Centre on Upper Gungate, officially listed as an ancient monument in 1973, evokes the days of the turnpikes and mail coaches. Outside Wilkinson's Store in Market Street, part of the top step of a mounting block, that served the building when it was the *King's Arms* and later the *Peel Arms*, remains preserved in the brickwork.

Number 10 Colehill dates from 1695 and was home to the Willington family until 1881, when it was bought by solicitors Robert Nevill and John Shaw for their offices. There are plenty of reminders of Georgian elegance, including a characteristic fanlight above the entrance to 11 Aldergate, one of many to be seen around the town, and the seven-bayed Manor House in Lichfield Street, rebuilt on

139 *Number 10, Colehill, built in 1695 and home to the Willington family until 1881, when it was bought as legal offices.*

140 *Sir Robert Peel statue and the old Town Hall. The great statesman looks out along Market Street from his granite pedestal outside the Town Hall.*

an earlier site that was home to the Vaughton family. On Church Street, the hotel named in honour of Colin Grazier was a Georgian townhouse before serving as municipal offices and police station. A tiny letterbox in the door of the Masonic Lodge at 29 Lichfield Street recalls the first days of postal deliveries. Before moving to Bolehall Manor, now a private club in Amington Road, William MacGregor lived in the 1830s vicarage in

Colehill occupied today by the Co-operative Society Milk Bar.

Sir Robert Peel, the great statesman, looks out along Market Street from his granite pedestal. The Victorian Peel Schools in Lichfield Street are still there. The earliest, at number 17, is now a betting shop, its Sydney Smirke-designed replacement across the road a dining room for Normid Housing Association's flats occupying the site of

141   *Peel School, Lichfield Street, designed by architect Sydney Smirke and now a dining room attached to Shannon's Mill sheltered housing flats.*

142 & 143 *Arms of the Townshend family above the archway of Holloway Lodge, built in 1810 by George, 2nd Marquis Townshend; and the base of a cast-iron Victorian water pump, Little Church Lane. Piped mains water became available in 1881, supplied from a reservoir at Glascote fed by a deep well at Hopwas.*

Thomas Cooke's and John Shannon's factory. The former National School building is still on College Lane.

The Bank House, home of the Savings Bank from 1845, is on Lady Bank. Opposite the Holloway Lodge entrance to the Castle Grounds, number 1 Lady Bank is the Brewery House. Built originally as a workhouse by Lord Middleton and Lord Weymouth, it was a brewery and then the Employment Exchange before becoming an annexe of the *Castle Hotel.*

Decorative horseshoes, some now badly weathered, on the ends of the projecting dripstone moulding above the arch of Holloway Lodge, are a reference to the Ferrers family crest. Facing Lady Bank, the arms of the Marmion family are carved on a stone shield. A matching shield on the other

144 *Gibbs and Canning's head of Edward VII, Argyle Street, one of many decorative terracotta pieces to be found in the area.*

145 *George Griffin clock, a reminder of the town's clockmaking tradition, above Griffin's former premises at 4 George Street.*

Gibbs and Canning's fine architectural terracotta can be seen to good effect on the frontage of the Co-operative Society's central premises in Colehill and the decorative arabesque tiles of 37 George Street. There is plenty more to be found in the area, particularly on the late Victorian and Edwardian period villas of Glascote, including a fine head of Edward VII in Argyle Street.

The angular Art Deco splendour of the former Electric Supply Company's building is in Church Street, its tower reduced in height from the days when it housed an air-raid siren and fire alert.

Above his former shop at 4 George Street is a timepiece by George Griffin, an emblem of the town's clockmaking tradition and a reminder to us that time does not stand still. It is all too easy to look back with rose-tinted disapproval at what has been lost in the development of modern Tamworth. Regret and nostalgia have their place and undoubtedly mistakes were made; some errors of judgement verge on civic vandalism. What we have lost is irreplaceable, but so too is what we have gained; and what we still have is often overlooked or undervalued. By embracing the new, by taking chances, Tamworth today is a thriving, living, growing blend of old and new, not some sanitised heritage town, dependent on tourists flocking to an artificially packaged 'Peel Country' or similar.

Celebrate Tamworth.

side of the gateway displays the Townshend arms. Inside the Castle Grounds, beyond the lodge gates, is Captain William Peel's trophy from the Crimean War, the anchor from a Russian ship transferred from its original home at Drayton Manor. Anchors also feature in the memorial to local hero Colin Grazier in St Editha's Square. The base of a Victorian cast-iron water pump still stands beside its stone trough in Little Church Lane. Part of Mrs Hutton's fountain, rescued and restored, provides a charming focal point for residents of the MacGregor Tithe housing development in Hospital Street.

SOURCES AND FURTHER READING

This bibliography is intended to highlight the main sources used in writing this history. I am indebted chiefly to Tamworth Castle Museum for access to their extensive deposit of primary printed and manuscript material including the town charters, the personal papers of the Ferrers family, the 'Peel Collection', electoral and municipal records, maps, deeds and other miscellaneous documents. Also to the Lichfield Record Office of Staffordshire and Stoke-on-Trent Archive Service for parish registers and to the local history collection held by Tamworth Central Library.

Main Sources

Transactions of the South Staffordshire Archaeological and Historical Society (various volumes 1968 onwards and particularly the reports by J. Gould)

Midland History volume 7 (1982) & volume 20 (1995) Dyer, C.C. and Cust, R.P. (eds.); volume 24 (1999) Röhrkasten, J. and Brown, D. (eds.)

Research Report (1970) by the County Planning and Development Office in conjunction with Tamworth Borough Council

Victoria County History of Staffordshire (1958) W. Page (ed.)

Secondary Sources and Further Reading

Staffordshire Historical Collections volume 4 (1883)

Bird V., *Staffordshire* (1974)

Comerford, P.J.M. and Adams, D.P., 'A History of the Comberford Family' (typescript in Tamworth Central Library local history collection)

Darby, H.C.and Terrett, I.B. (eds.), *The Domesday Geography of Midland England* (1971)

Dugdale, W., *The Antiquities of Warwickshire* (1765)

Erdeswick, S., *A Survey of Staffordshire* (1844)

Gelling, M., *The West Midlands in the Early Middle Ages* (1992)

Goodliffe, C.H., *A History of Tamworth Hospital* (1973)

Greenslade, M. W. and Stuart, D. G., *A History of Staffordshire* (2nd ed. 1998)

Harper, S., *Capturing Enigma* (1999)

Masefield, C., *Little Guide to Staffordshire* (1930)

Millward, R. and Robinson, A., *Landscapes of Britain: the West Midlands* (1971)

Mitchell, H.C., *Tamworth Parish Church* (1935)

Mitchell, H.C., *Tamworth Tower and Town* (1936)

Morrill, J. (ed.), *Reactions to the English Civil War* (1982)

Morris, John (ed.), *Domesday Book: Staffordshire* (1976)

Olleson, P., *The Tamworth Music Festival (Staffordshire Studies*: volume 5 1993)

Palliser, D.M., *Staffordshire Landscape* (1976)

Palmer, C.F.R., *History of the Town and Castle of Tamworth* (1845)

Palmer, C.F.R., *History and Antiquities of the Collegiate Church of Tamworth* (1871)

Pevsner, N., *Staffordshire* (1974)

Pointon, T.J., *Language of the Unheard: Civil Disorder in Staffordshire* (1991)

Sawyer, P., *Anglo-Saxon Charters* (1979)

Shaw, S., *The History and Antiquities of Staffordshire* (1798)

Shephard, D., *When the Chute Went Up* (1984)

Swift, M., 'Swift Look Round', selection of articles from the *Tamworth Herald* (Tamworth Central Library local history collection)

Wilson, D.M., *Archaeology of Anglo-Saxon England* (1976)

Wood, H., *Borough By Prescription* (1958)

Wood, H., *Guide to Tamworth Castle* (1954)

Wood, H., *Mediaeval Tamworth* (1971)

Wood, M., *Domesday* (1986)

Zaluckyj, S., *Mercia: the Anglo-Saxon Kingdom of Central England* (2001)

The websites of: www.tamworthcastle.freeserve.co.uk; www.genuki.org.uk

INDEX

Numbers in **bold** refer to illustration page numbers.

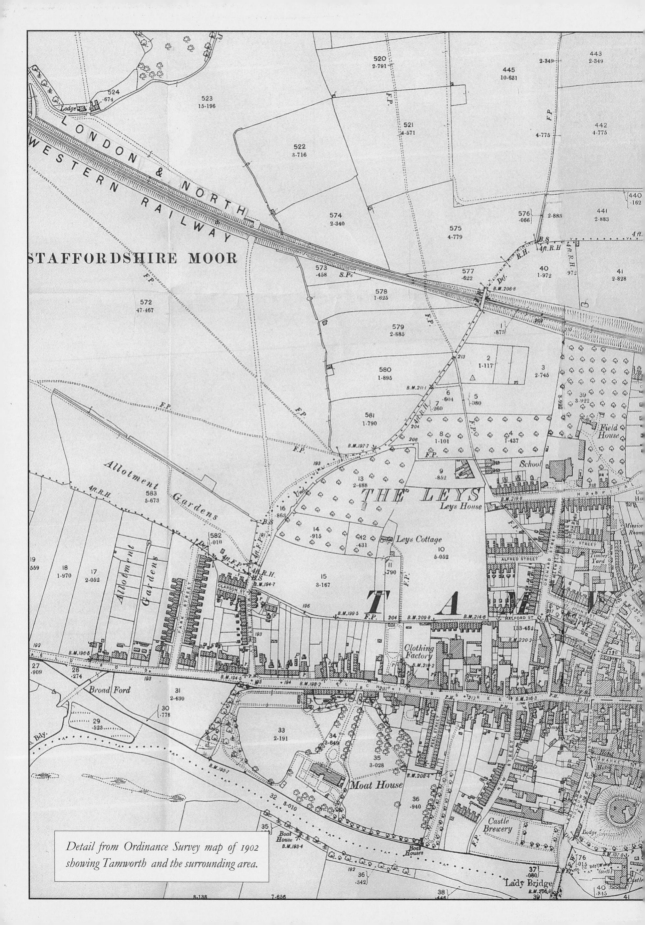

Detail from Ordinance Survey map of 1902 showing Tamworth and the surrounding area.